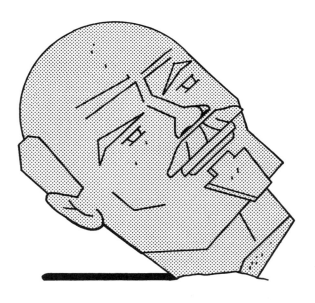

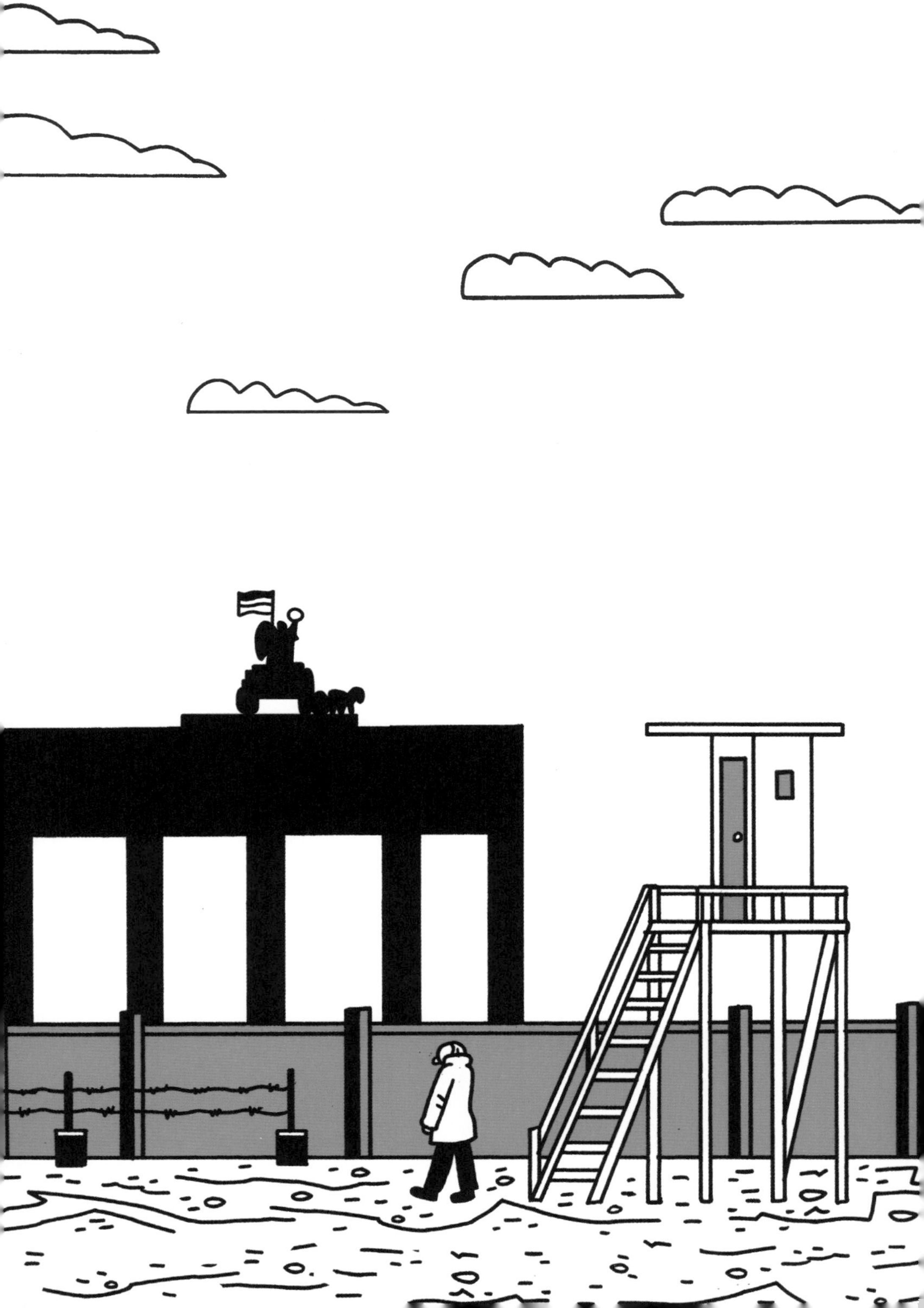

ACCIDENTAL CZAR

THE LIFE
AND LIES OF
VLADIMIR PUTIN

ANDREW S.
WEISS

ART BY **BRIAN "BOX"**
BROWN

:01
First Second
NEW YORK

First Second

Published by First Second • First Second is an imprint of Roaring Brook Press, a division of Holtzbrinck Publishing Holdings Limited Partnership • 120 Broadway, New York, NY 10271 • firstsecondbooks.com • Text © 2022 by Andrew S. Weiss • Illustrations © 2022 by Brian Brown • All rights reserved • Library of Congress Cataloging-in-Publication Data is available. • Our books may be purchased in bulk for promotional, educational, or business use. Please contact your local bookseller or the Macmillan Corporate and Premium Sales Department at (800) 221-7945 ext. 5442 or by email at MacmillanSpecialMarkets@macmillan.com. • First edition, 2022 • Edited by Mark Siegel and Alex Lu • Cover and interior book design by Sunny Lee, Madeline Morales, and Yan L. Moy • Production editing by Avia Perez • Research assistant: Aleksandar Vladicic • Penciled with 3H and 5H Staedtler pencils, erased with Pentel Hi-Polymer eraser, inked with Micron 08 pens, and colored in Photoshop. • Printed in Singapore • ISBN 978-1-250-76075-3 • 10 9 8 7 6 5 4 3 2 1 • Don't miss your next favorite book from First Second! For the latest updates go to firstsecondnewsletter.com and sign up for our enewsletter.

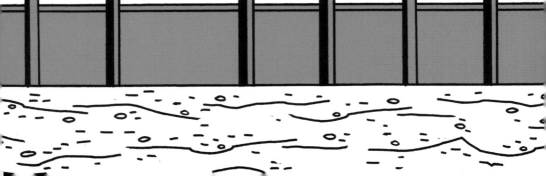

INTRODUCTION

"We demonstrated weakness, and the weak are beaten."
—**VLADIMIR PUTIN**, 2004

I'M ANDREW WEISS, AND I'M A RUSSIA GEEK.

I've spent most of the past thirty years thinking about who's up and who's down in the Kremlin. I've worked at the White House, the State Department, the Pentagon, and some of the world's top think tanks.

Nothing about my childhood suggested that I'd spend my life studying Russia. I grew up in Beverly Hills—we actually lived on Rodeo Drive. Many of my classmates' parents were famous actors or rock stars. One of the kids at Beverly Hills High School drove a Ferrari. I collected punk rock albums and started reading underground comic books. But in the end, all this was precisely why I would find Russia irresistible: It was the opposite of everything I'd known.

When I was thirteen years old, Ronald Reagan became president. All his tough talk about the Soviet Union being the Evil Empire sounded like dangerous fearmongering. And to a rebellious teenager eager to escape Southern California, it was hard to think of anything more exotic than the U.S.S.R. So on my first day of college in 1986, I threw myself into studying Russian language and literature as well as a now-extinct academic discipline known as Sovietology.

The U.S.S.R.'s final leader, a fatally flawed man named Mikhail Gorbachev, had become an international darling for trying to reform the Communist system. What he didn't appreciate was that brutality, dysfunction, and lies were actually the glue that kept the country together. By the time I arrived at Vladimir Putin's alma mater in Leningrad as an exchange student in 1989, the mighty U.S.S.R. was starting to fall apart.

I started working at the Pentagon in summer 1991, on the eve of a failed coup by Soviet hard-liners. Just months later, the Soviet Union disappeared, and America's relationship with Russia was transformed. The Pentagon was hungry for expertise on the twelve brand-new countries that had replaced the U.S.S.R., and I happened to be in the right place at the right time. At one point, the U.S. secretary of defense made a spur-of-the-moment decision to call his Russian counterpart, just to say hello, using a new secure telephone line. No one had made proper preparations, so I was hustled into his office at the last minute to be the translator. By the time I was thirty, I was going in and out of the Oval Office helping the president and his top advisers deal with their Russian counterparts.

Overconfident American officials kept saying the same thing to our new Russian friends: We were going to be partners, not adversaries. Yet Russia's leaders quickly found that it had been a lot more fun being America's enemy than our friend. With their country flat on its back, they resented being told to follow our lead. When the Russians did try to push back, they quickly realized how unequal our two countries' partnership actually was and that they were antagonizing the very people in the West who were paying billions of dollars to keep Russia from collapsing.

The West's hopes for Russia to make a successful transition to democracy and free markets turned out to be very unrealistic. Still, if you'd told me back then that a former mid-level KGB officer named Vladimir Putin, then forty-six years old, would be plucked from the back rooms of the Kremlin to run the country, I'd have told you to get your head examined. Yet there I was with President Bill Clinton on the August morning in 1999 when the Russians secretly informed him that Putin was going to be the country's next president. Even then, no one on Clinton's team could have imagined that Putin would eventually

dominate Russia like a modern-day czar, let alone become one of the world's most feared leaders.

Western experts like me would make plenty more mistakes in the decades that followed.

Even today, it's not always easy to understand what drives Putin. A lot of what we think we know about him is the product of pop psychology and misreadings of Russia's thousand-year-long history. Peeling all of that back is made harder by Putin's tough-guy theatrics (prancing around bare-chested on horseback, acting like a villain from a James Bond movie, etc.), which have helped him seem more clever—

and capable—than he actually is. As the political scientist Thomas Rid once wisely observed, "The Kremlin's rulers are particularly adept at gaming elements of this new age, or at the very least are good at getting everyone to talk about how good they are, which could be the most important trick of all."

Putin's resentment and grievances toward the West have never been far from the surface. Time and again, he's acted like a post-Soviet version of Oscar the Grouch, lecturing U.S. presidents and accusing them of hypocrisy, double standards, and attempts to humiliate Russia. At various points over the years, his finger-wagging has been occasionally punctuated by flashes of pragmatism and cooperation. But on the whole, his behavior has grown more belligerent over time.

Launching an undeclared war against neighboring Ukraine in 2014 would prove to be the most fateful decision of Putin's presidency. His obsession with Ukraine was not new; it had long been out in the open. But until that point, few people realized how far Putin was prepared to go to prevent Ukraine from being, in his phrasing, absorbed by the West, or how much his efforts would disrupt the global status quo.

To counteract Russia's post-2014 international isolation and to disrupt a U.S.-led pressure campaign, the Kremlin built bridges to far-right and populist Western politicians like Donald Trump. As a presidential candidate, Trump repaid the favor by showering Putin with compliments, including, astonishingly, about his brutal actions in Ukraine. The Kremlin interfered so blatantly on Trump's behalf in 2016 that Putin even cracked jokes about it before election day.

During Trump's presidency, Putin seemed to be having the time of his life. He was playing a crummy hand exceptionally well and enjoying something that he'd always craved: the world's undivided attention. As time went on, Putin's behavior got more and more brazen, bolstered by his own emotionalism and an undisguised belief in the West's deep, irreversible decline.

It was this same sense of self-confidence and opportunism that led Putin to launch a full-scale war against Ukraine in February 2022. Russia's unjustified invasion of a neighboring country was of course unprecedented—and it triggered an equally unprecedented outpouring of anger from democracies around the world. The fact that the whims of one man had caused this calamity was lost on no one. But conspicuously missing from the resulting conversation about Putin was much awareness that the West's problems with Russia go far beyond its leader's uncompromising, hard-edged tactics.

To date, there has been far too little discussion of the intense grievances that have piled up on both sides—not to mention the growing risks that these conflicts could potentially spin out of control.

If we're going to deal effectively with Putin, we need to do better. We need to understand his motivations, along with the heavy burden of history that helped shape them. We need to see the parts of a man who is in many ways ordinary, even if the problems he has created are often extraordinary.

And that's why I wrote this book.

CHAPTER
1
SUPER SPY

LENINGRAD, MID-1980S

VLADIMIR PUTIN, THEN A THIRTY-SOMETHING KGB OFFICER, MADE A STARTLING CONFESSION TO HIS BEST FRIEND.

SOME PUNK ON THE SUBWAY WAS BUGGING ME SO I BEAT THE CRAP OUT OF HIM.

THE FIGHT LEFT PUTIN WITH A BROKEN ARM—AND JEOPARDIZED HIS CAREER PATH AT THE KGB, WHERE HE WAS ALREADY KNOWN AS A HOTHEAD.

AT THE TIME, HE WAS ENROLLED AT AN ELITE KGB TRAINING PROGRAM AT THE FAMED RED BANNER INSTITUTE DEEP IN A FOREST OUTSIDE MOSCOW.

PUTIN HAD BEEN WAITING A DECADE TO GET INTO THE PROGRAM, TOILING IN THE BOWELS OF THE KGB IN THE MEANTIME.

IN MOSCOW THEY WON'T UNDERSTAND THIS. I'M WORRIED THERE ARE GOING TO BE CONSEQUENCES.

THE SCREW-UP WRECKED HIS LIFELONG DREAM OF A GLAMOROUS FOREIGN ASSIGNMENT RUNNING SPY NETWORKS AND STEALING SECRETS. HE LEFT THE PROGRAM AFTER ONLY ONE YEAR.

4

BUT WE'RE GETTING AHEAD OF OURSELVES. LET'S GO BACK TO PUTIN'S ROOTS IN LENINGRAD (NOW ST. PETERSBURG).

PUTIN'S PARENTS BARELY SURVIVED THE NAZI BLOCKADE DURING WWII.

AROUND A MILLION PEOPLE IN THE CITY DIED DURING THE SIEGE, MOSTLY FROM HUNGER AND COLD.

PEOPLE ATE THINGS LIKE GLUE, PINE NEEDLES, AND LEATHER BELTS TO SURVIVE.

PUTIN NEVER MET HIS OLDER BROTHER, WHO WAS TAKEN AWAY FROM THE FAMILY DURING THE WAR TO SAVE HIM FROM HUNGER. HE DIED OF DIPHTHERIA...

...AND WAS BURIED IN A MASS GRAVE.

PUTIN'S FATHER WAS SERIOUSLY WOUNDED IN COMBAT. ON THE DAY HE RETURNED HOME FROM THE HOSPITAL, HE SAW HIS WIFE BEING TAKEN AWAY WITH THE CORPSES TO BE BURIED.

SHE'S STILL ALIVE!!

SHE'S NOT GOING TO MAKE IT. SHE'LL DIE ALONG THE WAY.

SHE'S STILL BREATHING!

I'M TAKING HER HOME!

PUTIN WAS BORN SEVEN YEARS AFTER THE WAR. AS A KID, HE CHASED RATS AROUND HIS RUN-DOWN APARTMENT BUILDING JUST FOR FUN.

ONE DAY, HE LEARNED AN IMPORTANT LIFE LESSON.

HE DROVE A RAT INTO THE CORNER. IT HAD NOWHERE LEFT TO RUN.

YOU LITTLE BASTARD!

SUDDENLY, THE RAT LASHED OUT AND THREW ITSELF AT PUTIN.

HE WAS SURPRISED AND FRIGHTENED.

NOW THE RAT WAS CHASING HIM.

PUTIN'S EARLY YEARS WERE SPENT GETTING INTO TROUBLE. HE WAS A HORRIBLE STUDENT AND A STREET HOOLIGAN.

BUT STUDYING GERMAN...

...AND JUDO INSPIRED HIM TO GET HIS LIFE BACK ON TRACK.

PUTIN WAS ALSO MOTIVATED BY HIS INTENSE LOVE FOR SOVIET POP CULTURE GLORIFYING THE KGB...

SPECIFICALLY, THE BLOCKBUSTER MOVIE *THE SWORD AND THE SHIELD* AND THE PULP SPY NOVELS THAT WERE THE BASIS FOR THE SMASH TV MINISERIES *17 MOMENTS OF SPRING.*

HE MODELED HIMSELF AFTER TWO FICTIONAL KGB SECRET AGENTS, BELOV AND STIERLITZ, AND TRIED TO WORM HIS WAY INTO THE KGB.

THEY'RE SENDING ME BEHIND ENEMY LINES.

9

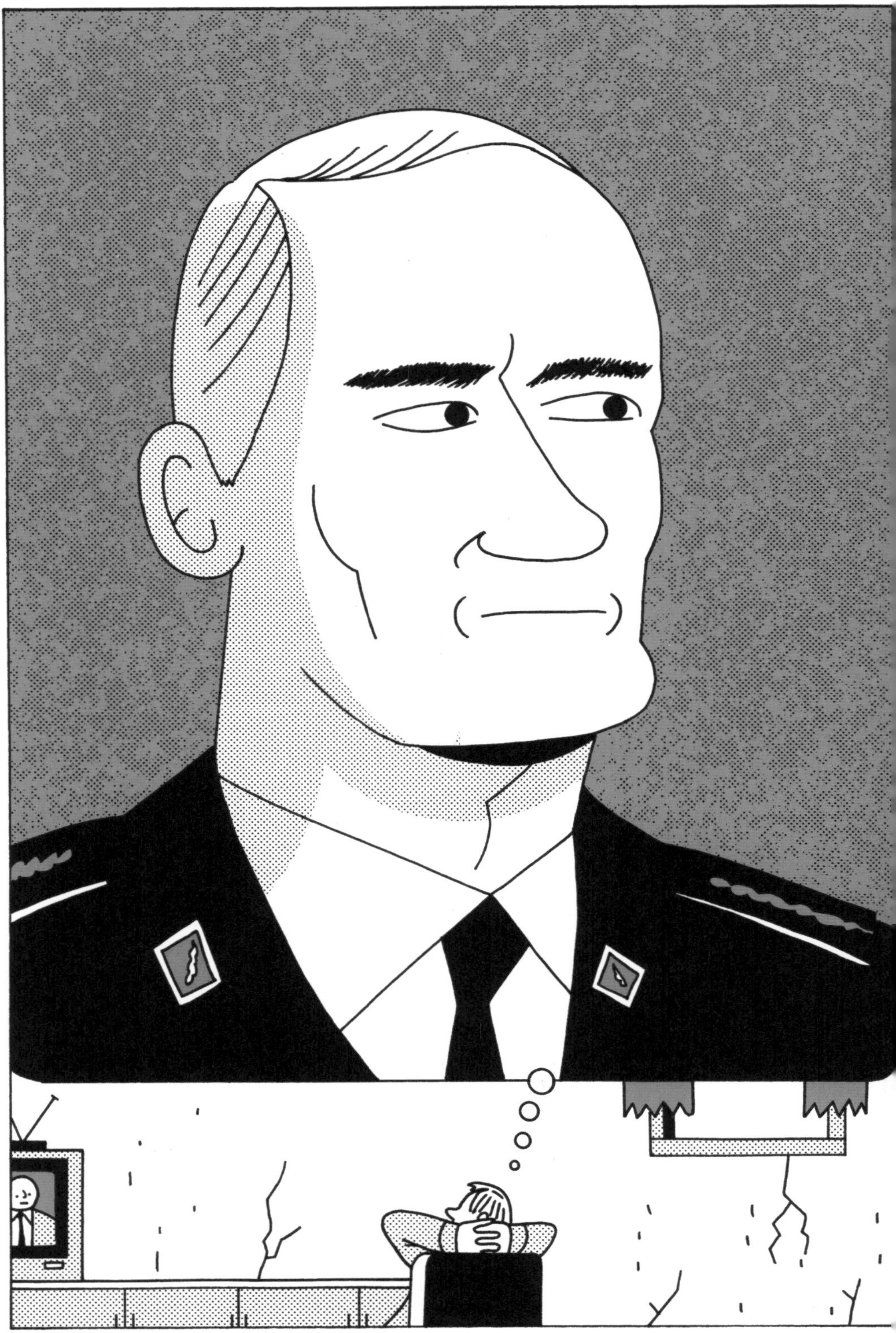

IN 1966, PUTIN WAS IN NINTH GRADE. HE HAD MADE UP HIS MIND THAT HE WANTED A CAREER IN THE KGB. SO HE WALKED UP TO ITS MAMMOTH HEADQUARTERS BUILDING IN LENINGRAD.

I WANT TO WORK FOR YOU.

FIRST OF ALL, WE DON'T TAKE WALK-INS.

YOU CAN ONLY END UP HERE AFTER SERVING IN THE ARMY OR STUDYING AT SOME KIND OF COLLEGE.

WHAT KIND OF COLLEGE?

ANY KIND!

WELL, WHAT WOULD YOU RECOMMEND?

GET A LAW DEGREE!

BEAT IT, KID!

FROM THAT MOMENT ON, PUTIN SET HIS SIGHTS ON GOING TO THE BEST LAW SCHOOL IN HIS HOMETOWN.

HIS PARENTS OBJECTED. THEY THOUGHT HE WAS BEING UNREALISTIC.

LENINGRAD STATE UNIVERSITY DID NOT TAKE MANY STUDENTS FROM WORKING-CLASS FAMILIES.

BUT HE PERSISTED AND BEAT THE ODDS.

THROUGHOUT HIS COLLEGE YEARS, PUTIN NURTURED THE FANTASY THAT THE OFFICER HE HAD MET IN NINTH GRADE HADN'T FORGOTTEN HIM.

HE DAYDREAMED THAT THE KGB WOULD BECKON HIM TO SIGN UP.

DURING HIS SENIOR YEAR, PUTIN'S DREAM CAME TRUE. HE GOT A MYSTERIOUS REQUEST FOR A MEETING AT THE LAW DEPARTMENT'S OFFICES ABOUT HIS FUTURE PLANS.

THE PERSON SHOWED UP TWENTY MINUTES LATE.

AM I BEING PRANKED HERE?

SORRY, I'M LATE...

SUCH A PIG.

THE RECRUITER WAS GUARDED AND IMPRECISE.

WE'RE TALKING ABOUT YOUR FUTURE ASSIGNMENT...DON'T WANT TO SPECIFY WHERE.

YOU'VE GOT A LOT OF TIME IN FRONT OF YOU, VOLODYA.* HOW WOULD YOU FEEL, IN GENERAL AND ON THE WHOLE, IF SOMEONE OFFERED YOU A JOB IN THE SECURITY ORGANS?

*A FRIENDLY NICKNAME FOR VLADIMIR

PUTIN ENTERED THE KGB IN 1975.

YET, INSTEAD OF BEING GROOMED FOR FOREIGN POSTINGS WITH THE JAMES BOND—STYLE EXCITEMENT HE CRAVED...

...PUTIN SPENT THE NEXT TEN YEARS IN MOSTLY MIND-NUMBING, LOW-LEVEL JOBS—TOILING IN THE HR DEPARTMENT...

TAKE THIS UPSTAIRS.

...KEEPING TABS ON THE ARTISTIC COMMUNITY TO CHECK FOR ANY IDEOLOGICAL DEVIATIONS...

...SHADOWING FOREIGN STUDENTS AND TOURISTS...

...AND WORKING IN COUNTERINTELLIGENCE, WHERE HE SEARCHED FOR SPIES WITHIN THE RANKS OF THE KGB.

ACCORDING TO MAJOR GENERAL OLEG KALUGIN, HEAD OF THE LENINGRAD KGB OFFICE AT THE TIME:

"OUR 3,000-PERSON KGB OFFICE IN LENINGRAD CONTINUED TO HARASS DISSIDENTS AND ORDINARY CITIZENS..."

"...AS WELL AS TO HUNT FUTILELY FOR SPIES."

"BUT I CAN TRULY SAY THAT NEARLY ALL OF WHAT WE DID WAS USELESS."

IN THE TWENTY YEARS BEFORE MY ARRIVAL IN LENINGRAD, THE LOCAL KGB HADN'T CAUGHT ONE SPY.

DESPITE THE EXPENDITURE OF MILLIONS OF RUBLES AND TENS OF THOUSANDS OF MAN-HOURS.

PUTIN MADE NO IMPRESSION ON HIM.

HE WAS A NOBODY.

FOLLOWING THE FIGHT ON THE SUBWAY, PUTIN WAS SENT TO DRESDEN, A DREARY BACKWATER, INSTEAD OF A MORE IMPORTANT POSTING FOR A FLUENT GERMAN SPEAKER.

EAST GERMANY, 1985

THE REAL ACTION WAS IN PLACES LIKE THE KGB OFFICE IN EAST BERLIN, WHICH HAD ROUGHLY A THOUSAND EMPLOYEES.

THE MOST CUSHY JOBS WERE IN WEST GERMANY, BUT THEY WERE RESERVED FOR PEOPLE WITH FAMILY CONNECTIONS OR SPECIALIZED SKILLS.

BY CONTRAST, THE KGB OFFICE IN DRESDEN WAS JUST A SMALL RESIDENTIAL VILLA STAFFED BY SIX.

IN DRESDEN, PUTIN WAS GIVEN MUNDANE ASSIGNMENTS...

LIAISING WITH THE EAST GERMAN INTELLIGENCE SERVICE, THE STASI.

AND TRACKING U.S. TROOPS IN WEST GERMANY.

PUTIN'S TEAM TRIED TO IDENTIFY PEOPLE WHO WERE TRAVELING TO WEST GERMANY AND MIGHT BE WILLING TO REPORT ON WHAT THEY SAW. THEY ALSO TRIED TO ENTICE FOREIGN STUDENTS INTO SERVING AS "ILLEGALS" IN THE U.S.

IN OTHER WORDS, SLEEPER AGENTS WITH ASSUMED IDENTITIES, LIKE THE PHILIP AND ELIZABETH JENNINGS CHARACTERS ON *THE AMERICANS*.

RECRUITMENT EFFORTS WERE HAMPERED BY THE KGB'S LACK OF RESOURCES. THEY COULDN'T MAKE THE NOTION OF SPYING FOR MOSCOW FINANCIALLY COMPELLING.

PUTIN WAS A COG INSIDE A GIANT MACHINE. THE KGB WAS A STATE WITHIN A STATE.

IT MADE PUTIN UNCOMFORTABLE THAT EAST GERMANY WAS A POLICE STATE AKIN TO THE USSR OF THE 1950S.

THE SECRET POLICE AND THEIR INFORMANTS WERE EVERYWHERE.

PUTIN AND HIS FIVE COLLEAGUES UNDERSTOOD THEIR SITUATION PERFECTLY WELL. THEIR ASSIGNMENTS AND DESK WORK WERE BASICALLY MEANINGLESS.

NO ONE IN MOSCOW WAS PAYING MUCH ATTENTION.

BACK HOME, GORBACHEV'S PERESTROIKA AND GLASNOST POLICIES OF LIBERALIZING THE COMMUNIST SYSTEM HAD OPENED A PANDORA'S BOX.

A CHAIN REACTION OF CRISES EXPLODED ACROSS THE WARSAW PACT AND INSIDE THE SOVIET UNION ITSELF.

THE TOP SOVIET LEADERSHIP AND KGB QUICKLY LOST THEIR ABILITY TO CONTROL EVENTS.

PUTIN AND HIS WORK BUDDIES RESPONDED TO THE PRESSURES ALL TOO SENSIBLY. THEY DRANK TONS OF BEER AND PACKED ON THE POUNDS.

ANOTHER ROUND?

DA!

BEHIND THE SCENES, EAST GERMANY'S HARD-LINE LEADERS RESISTED PLEAS FROM GORBACHEV TO LIBERALIZE LIKE OTHER NATIONS BEHIND THE IRON CURTAIN SUCH AS POLAND AND HUNGARY.

THE LEADERSHIP OF EAST GERMANY AND THE STASI CONSISTED OF TRUE BELIEVERS IN THE COMMUNIST SYSTEM, NOT WOULD-BE REFORMERS. THAT BLINDED THEM TO PENT-UP FRUSTRATION INSIDE THEIR COUNTRY.

A NONVIOLENT EAST GERMAN GRASSROOTS MOVEMENT INSPIRED BY DR. MARTIN LUTHER KING JR. PUSHED FOR CHANGE.

THE UNRAVELING OF EAST GERMANY CAME QUICKLY IN THE SUMMER AND AUTUMN OF 1989.

A LARGE GROUP OF EAST GERMANS MADE A DASH TO NEARBY HUNGARY. HUNGARY'S LEADERS HAD OPENED A CRACK IN THE IRON CURTAIN. SUDDENLY THEY HAD AN ESCAPE ROUTE TO A LIFE OF FREEDOM IN WEST GERMANY.

SOON 200,000 EAST GERMANS WERE ON THE MOVE. THOUSANDS CAMPED OUT IN FRONT OF THE WEST GERMAN EMBASSIES IN PRAGUE AND WARSAW.

EAST AND WEST GERMANY CUT A DEAL. PEOPLE STRANDED IN HUNGARY, POLAND, AND CZECHOSLOVAKIA COULD LEAVE FOR THE WEST. BUT THEY HAD TO TRAVEL IN SEALED TRAINS ACROSS EAST GERMANY...

...SO THE GOVERNMENT COULD CLAIM THEY WERE ACTUALLY BEING EXPELLED.

THE DEAL TURNED TO CHAOS AS THE TRAINS REACHED DRESDEN.

EAST GERMAN CITIZENS, SENSING THIS WAS THEIR LAST CHANCE TO MAKE A RUN FOR IT, TRIED TO BUY THEIR WAY ONTO THE TRAINS PASSING THROUGH THE CITY.

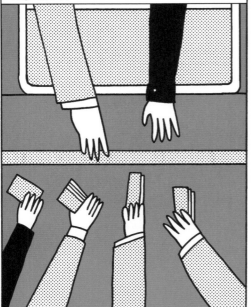

THEY PROTESTED OUTSIDE THE TRAIN STATION. THEY BLOCKED THE TRACKS.

chts DEUTSC
FREIHEIT!

DEUTSCHLAND einig TERLAND

hregen in die e Traufe?

23

EAST GERMAN LEADER ERICH HONECKER WAS IMPRESSED BY HOW CHINESE COMRADES HAD HANDLED SIMILAR PROTESTS IN TIANANMEN SQUARE JUST A FEW MONTHS EARLIER.

HE DECIDED TO STAGE A CRACKDOWN. THE PROTESTS IN DRESDEN HAD TO BE STOPPED.

THE STAGE WAS SET FOR A CONFRONTATION.

ON THE EVENING OF OCTOBER 4, THE DRESDEN TRAIN STATION BECAME A BATTLE ZONE.

POLICE BEAT THE PROTESTERS AND ATTACKED THEM WITH WATER CANNONS. THEY FOUGHT BACK.

TROOPS WITH MACHINE GUNS ARRIVED IN LEIPZIG, A NEARBY CITY. HONECKER PLANNED A VIOLENT TIANANMEN–STYLE ASSAULT TO SNUFF OUT THE PROTEST MOVEMENT.

AS THE PROTESTS SWELLED, CLERGY AND ACTIVISTS EMBRACED CIVIL DISOBEDIENCE AND TRIED TO NEGOTIATE WITH THE AUTHORITIES.

BUT BY SEALING THE BORDERS, EAST GERMANY'S LEADERS HAD CREATED A PRESSURE COOKER.

ONE MONTH LATER, THE BERLIN WALL FELL. IT WAS ACTUALLY AN ACCIDENT CAUSED BY A STASI OFFICER SPOOKED BY THE FEARLESSNESS OF THE DEMONSTRATORS.

WESTERNERS SAW ONLY JOYFUL SCENES.

PUTIN KNEW BETTER.

EAST GERMANY HAD NARROWLY AVOIDED A BLOODBATH.

CHAPTER
2

RIDING HIGH

PUTIN'S LARGER-THAN-LIFE, CARTOONISH IMAGE DOMINATES MUCH OF OUR COLLECTIVE CONSCIOUSNESS AND POLITICAL DISCOURSE TODAY.

HE SEEMS LIKE THE PERFECT MADE-FOR-TV VILLAIN.

A CUNNING INTELLIGENCE OPERATIVE WITH A STRATEGY FOR GLOBAL DOMINATION...

...WHO LEAVES A MESSY TRAIL OF BLOOD AND DESTRUCTION IN HIS WAKE.

PUTINOLOGISTS LOVE TO SAY THAT HE IS ALWAYS UP TO SOMETHING, PLOTTING AND SCHEMING TO DESTROY AMERICA, HIS SWORN ENEMY SINCE HE JOINED THE KGB.

IT SEEMS LIKE THE GUY MUST BE TEN FEET TALL.

ACTUALLY, HE'S ABOUT THE SAME HEIGHT AS NAPOLEON, FIVE FOOT SEVEN.

THAT EXPLAINS WHY HE OFTEN WEARS ELEVATOR SHOES.

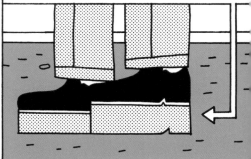

OVER THE COURSE OF 20+ YEARS IN POWER, PUTIN'S BEHAVIOR HAS GONE THROUGH MANY DIFFERENT CYCLES.

HELSINKI   HELSINKI

PUTIN'S RELATIONSHIP WITH AMERICA HASN'T ALWAYS BEEN SO BLACK AND WHITE.

HE'S OFTEN BALANCED TOUGH (OKAY, OBNOXIOUS) TALK...

SOMETIMES IT'S NECESSARY TO BE LONELY IN ORDER TO PROVE THAT YOU ARE RIGHT.

...WITH A DESIRE FOR SOME FORM OF PARTNERSHIP OR COOPERATION WITH THE WEST THAT HE FELT SERVED RUSSIA'S LONG-TERM INTERESTS.

THAT PRAGMATIC SIDE IS NOWHERE TO BE SEEN THESE DAYS, BUT...

...HE WAS THE FIRST LEADER TO CALL THE WHITE HOUSE AFTER THE 9/11 ATTACKS.

WE'VE HEARD THE NEWS.

WE'LL SUPPORT ANY U.S. ATTACKS ON AL-QAEDA AND THE TALIBAN.

PRESIDENT BUSH WAS NOT REACHABLE ON AIR FORCE ONE THAT DAY, SO PUTIN SPOKE WITH CONDOLEEZZA RICE.

SHE WAS SAFE IN THE PRESIDENTIAL EMERGENCY OPERATIONS CENTER UNDER THE EAST WING OF THE WHITE HOUSE.

RUSSIA WILL NOT INCREASE OUR MILITARY READINESS DESPITE THE U.S. MOVING TO DEFCON 3.

YOU UNDERSTAND THAT DURING THE COLD WAR, THE INCREASE WOULD'VE BEEN DONE AUTOMATICALLY. INSTEAD, WE'VE CANCELED OUR EXERCISES AND BROUGHT ALERT LEVELS DOWN.

PUTIN SPOKE DIRECTLY TO THE PRESIDENT ON SEPTEMBER 12.

GOOD WILL TRIUMPH OVER EVIL. I WANT YOU TO KNOW THAT IN THIS STRUGGLE WE WILL STAND TOGETHER.

PUTIN ENDORSED THE HUGELY CONTROVERSIAL STRING OF U.S. AND NATO BASES INSIDE THE FORMER SOVIET UNION.

LARGE BASES FOR U.S. AIRCRAFT AND PERSONNEL WERE BUILT IN UZBEKISTAN...

...AND KYRGYZSTAN, RIGHT AT AFGHANISTAN'S DOORSTEP.

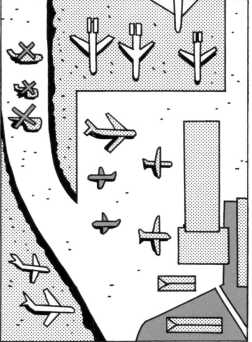

PUTIN'S FORWARD-LEANING RESPONSE TO 9/11 GAVE HIM A TASTE OF WHAT IT WAS LIKE TO BE AMERICA'S BUDDY.

HE RODE AROUND GEORGE W. BUSH'S RANCH IN A PICKUP TRUCK.

HE WENT ON A FISHING VACATION WITH BUSH AND HIS FATHER IN KENNEBUNKPORT.

BUSH EVEN INVITED PUTIN TO SIT IN ON A SESSION OF THE CIA'S PRESIDENTIAL DAILY BRIEF. PUTIN AUTOGRAPHED HIS COPY OF THE BRIEFING BOOK BEFORE HANDING IT BACK OVER TO U.S. OFFICIALS.

OF COURSE, PUTIN HAD HIS OWN MOTIVES FOR DOING THIS STUFF.

HIS PRIORITIES AT THE TIME WERE ALL DOMESTIC. HE WANTED TO REVIVE A BATTERED ECONOMY...

...AND RE-CENTRALIZE THE POWERS OF THE RUSSIAN GOVERNMENT AFTER THE CALAMITOUS 1990S.

EXCHANGE

STABLE RELATIONS WITH THE WEST WERE AN IMPORTANT ELEMENT OF ACHIEVING THESE GOALS.

HE ALSO WANTED TO GET AMERICA OFF HIS BACK ABOUT THINGS LIKE SEIZING CONTROL OF THE MEDIA...

...OR FIGHTING A BLOODY WAR IN CHECHNYA, A PREDOMINANTLY MUSLIM BREAKAWAY PROVINCE.

BREAKING NEWS: AN ARREST WARRANT WAS ISSUED FOR THE BILLIONAIRE OWNER OF RUSSIA'S MAIN TV CHANNEL.

GOOD NEWS TODAY FROM THE RUSSIAN MILITARY. THE LIBERATION OF THE CHECHEN CAPITAL, GROZNY, HAS BEEN COMPLETED.

ALONG THE WAY, PUTIN BECAME CHUMMY WITH LEADERS OF THE U.K....

...GERMANY...

...ITALY, AND OTHER COUNTRIES.

HE CLEARLY WANTED TO BE PART OF THE BIG GUY CLUB AND JOIN THE WEST.

EVEN THOUGH HE KNEW FULL WELL THAT HE'D BE ENTERING FROM A POSITION OF WEAKNESS.

BUT PUTIN'S RESENTMENT OF THE WEST AND NOTORIOUS THIN SKIN WERE NEVER FAR FROM THE SURFACE. ANGRY SPEECHES TRIGGERED PERIODIC ALARM BELLS ABOUT THE POSSIBLE BEGINNINGS OF A NEW COLD WAR.

AFTER THE DISASTROUS U.S. INVASION OF IRAQ IN 2003, HE GOT ANGRY AT THE WORLD'S SOLE SUPERPOWER FOR IGNORING RUSSIA'S OBJECTIONS.

HE COMPLAINED REPEATEDLY THAT U.S. LEADERS WERE OUT OF CONTROL.

COMRADE WOLF KNOWS WHOM TO EAT, HE EATS WITHOUT LISTENING, AND HE'S CLEARLY NOT GOING TO LISTEN TO ANYONE.

MUNICH, FEBRUARY 2007

[THE WORLD HAS NOW] ONE CENTER OF AUTHORITY, ONE CENTER OF FORCE, ONE CENTER OF DECISION-MAKING. IT IS A WORLD WHERE THERE IS ONE MASTER. ONE SOVEREIGN.

AND, OF COURSE, THIS IS EXTREMELY DANGEROUS. IT RESULTS IN THE FACT THAT NO ONE FEELS SAFE. I WANT TO EMPHASIZE THIS—NO ONE FEELS SAFE!

JOHN McCAIN

MOSCOW, MAY 2007, VICTORY DAY

WE HAVE A DUTY TO REMEMBER THAT THE CAUSES OF ANY WAR LIE ABOVE ALL IN THE MISTAKES AND MISCALCULATIONS OF PEACETIME.

PUTIN STOPPED HOLDING BACK. HE DREW A PATENTLY OFFENSIVE COMPARISON BETWEEN THE U.S. AND NAZI GERMANY.

THESE NEW THREATS, JUST AS UNDER THE THIRD REICH, SHOW THE SAME CONTEMPT FOR HUMAN LIFE.

AND THE SAME ASPIRATION TO ESTABLISH AN EXCLUSIVE DIKTAT OVER THE WORLD.

BUT WHAT PUTIN REALLY WANTED, AND STILL WANTS, IS NO MYSTERY: FOR RUSSIA TO BE A PART OF THE BOARD OF DIRECTORS THAT SETS THE RULES FOR THE REST OF THE WORLD.

HE ALSO WANTS A SPHERE OF INFLUENCE IN RUSSIA'S BACKYARD.

THAT MEANS NO MEMBERSHIP IN NATO OR THE EUROPEAN UNION FOR COUNTRIES LIKE UKRAINE OR GEORGIA.

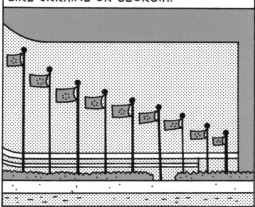

PUTIN TOLD THE U.S. AMBASSADOR PRIVATELY:

YOU AMERICANS NEED TO LISTEN MORE.

YOU CAN'T HAVE IT YOUR WAY ANYMORE.

WE CAN HAVE EFFECTIVE RELATIONS...

...BUT NOT JUST ON YOUR TERMS.

INSTEAD OF TAKING HIM SERIOUSLY, THE BUSH ADMINISTRATION BLEW PUTIN OFF...

...AND DIDN'T REGISTER HOW QUICKLY HE WAS RECONSTITUTING HARD POWER TOOLS LIKE THE MILITARY AND INTELLIGENCE SERVICES.

IN 2006, THE WHITE HOUSE ACTED LIKE RUSSIA WAS LITTLE MORE THAN A GOOD PLACE FOR A REFUELING STOP FOR AIR FORCE ONE WHEN BUSH WAS FLYING TO VIETNAM.

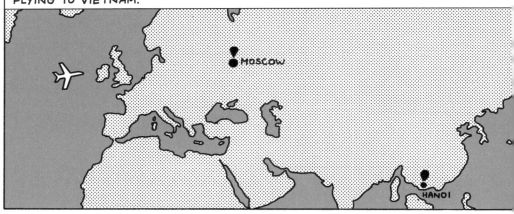

MOSCOW

HANOI

INSTEAD OF DRIVING INTO TOWN TO MEET PUTIN AT THE KREMLIN, OVERBEARING WHITE HOUSE STAFF INSISTED ON DOING THE MEETING AT THE AIRPORT.

MEANWHILE, SOMETHING ELSE VERY IMPORTANT HAD HAPPENED: THE RUSSIAN ELITE HAD GOTTEN RICH, UNBELIEVABLY FILTHY RICH. GLOBAL COMMODITY PRICES SOARED DURING MOST OF THE FIRST DECADE OF PUTIN'S REIGN.

WITH OIL HITTING LEVELS ABOVE $100 A BARREL, MOSCOW SUDDENLY HAD MORE BILLIONAIRES THAN NEW YORK CITY.

THE LEVEL OF AFFLUENCE WAS JARRING.

THE FLASHY, CONSPICUOUS CONSUMPTION REMINDED ME OF BEVERLY HILLS OR DUBAI (WITH MORE SNOW).

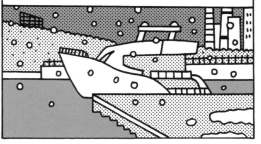

THE RUSSIAN ELITE STARTED ACTING LIKE THE SAUDIS, WHO, AS ONE FORMER U.S. AMBASSADOR ONCE JOKED, DIVIDE PEOPLE OF THE WORLD INTO TWO CATEGORIES:

FELLOW SAUDIS

POTENTIAL EMPLOYEES

GEORGE H. W. BUSH

DICK CHENEY

IN 2007, PUTIN FLEW TO GUATEMALA TO PERSUADE THE INTERNATIONAL OLYMPIC COMMITTEE TO LET HIM HOST THE WINTER GAMES IN SOCHI.

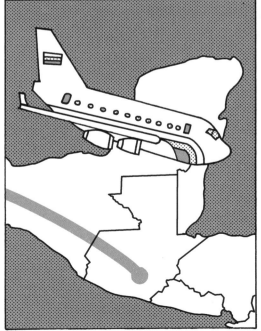

FLUSH WITH CASH, HE BARELY BATTED AN EYE AT THE $55 BILLION PRICE TAG.

GUATEMALA

TWO YEARS LATER, PUTIN PROMISED TO SPEND TENS OF BILLIONS MORE TO HOST THE 2018 FIFA WORLD CUP.

THE TEAM THAT PUT TOGETHER THE BRITISH BID FOR THE TOURNAMENT WAS FURIOUS. THEY HIRED A FORMER INTELLIGENCE OPERATIVE TO INVESTIGATE WHETHER THE RUSSIANS HAD PAID BRIBES TO FIFA, THE NOTORIOUSLY CORRUPT GOVERNING BODY OF SOCCER.

THEIR INVESTIGATOR WAS NONE OTHER THAN CHRISTOPHER STEELE, WHO WOULD LATER COMPILE THE INFAMOUS TRUMP DOSSIER.

STEELE'S FINDINGS WERE SHARED WITH THE FBI, LEADING TO CRIMINAL INDICTMENTS OF FIFA'S LEADERSHIP AND A LONG-TERM RELATIONSHIP BETWEEN STEELE AND U.S. LAW ENFORCEMENT.

THE QUEST TO HOST THE OLYMPICS AND THE WORLD CUP FIT PERFECTLY WITH PUTIN'S VANITY.

HE UNDERSTANDABLY CRAVED INTERNATIONAL RECOGNITION OF RUSSIA'S MANY POST-2000 ACHIEVEMENTS.

HE ALSO LIKED OFFERING BREAD AND CIRCUSES TO THE MASSES.

RUSSIAN OLIGARCHS KNEW WHAT WAS EXPECTED OF THEM AND QUICKLY PLEDGED MONEY FOR BIG CONSTRUCTION PROJECTS.

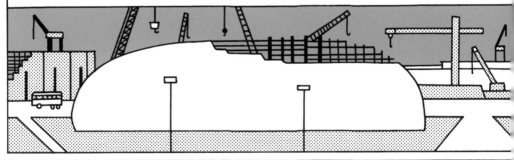

UNLIKE THE ONCE MIGHTY OLIGARCHS WHO HAD LORDED OVER THE KREMLIN IN THE '90S, FIGURES LIKE OLEG DERIPASKA AND VIKTOR VEKSELBERG FIGURED OUT THE WAY TO GET EVEN RICHER WAS TO DO FAVORS FOR THE KREMLIN AND KEEP THEIR NOSES OUT OF POLITICS.

I HAPPENED TO BE IN MOSCOW MOON-LIGHTING FOR THE RAND CORPORATION DURING THE WORST WEEK OF THE GLOBAL FINANCIAL CRISIS IN 2008. LEHMAN BROTHERS AND MY OWN FIRM (AIG) HAD EXPLODED.

CRAP.

THE WORLD'S BIGGEST BANKS WERE CHOOSING BETWEEN A SIMILAR FATE OR ACCEPTING GOVERNMENT BAILOUTS.

WALL ST. OVERDRAFTED OUR ECONOMY

HOLD BANKS TO ACCOUNT!!

I MET ONE-ON-ONE THAT WEEK WITH NEARLY ALL OF RUSSIA'S FAMOUS OLIGARCHS.

VIKTOR VEKSELBERG

MIKHAIL FRIDMAN

PETR AVEN

KREMLIN OFFICIALS WERE DISBELIEVING WHEN I WARNED THEM THAT THE ENTIRE U.S. FINANCIAL SYSTEM WAS ON THE VERGE OF COLLAPSE.

I'M SERIOUS.

SEPTEMBER 2008 TURNED OUT TO BE A KEY MOMENT IN TERMS OF REMOVING THE WEST'S AURA OF INVINCIBILITY.

HAHA!

A KREMLIN OFFICIAL

EVEN THOUGH PUTIN HAD TURNED MOSCOW INTO THE GLITTERING PLEASURE PALACE OF A RUSSIAN PETRO-STATE, THE CRISIS HIT THE COUNTRY HARD. OIL PRICES COLLAPSED.

NONETHELESS, PUTIN'S OLDEST COLLEAGUES WERE REALLY MOVING UP IN THE WORLD.

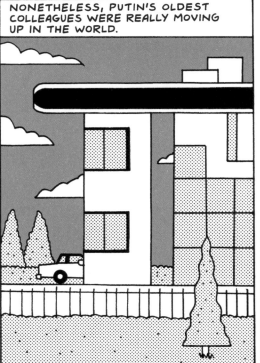

AS A RUSSIAN FRIEND OF MINE ONCE QUIPPED, "MOST OF THESE GUYS SHOULD HAVE TOPPED OUT RUNNING STOLEN RESTAURANTS IN THE 1990S..."

"...INSTEAD, THEY'RE RUNNING THE COUNTRY."

AFTER PUTIN'S RISE TO POWER, PEOPLE FROM THE SECURITY SERVICES BECAME MUCH MORE AMBITIOUS.

DRESDEN

PREVIOUSLY MID-LEVEL INTEL OFFICERS WHO HAPPENED TO KNOW PUTIN (OR SOMEONE WHO KNEW SOMEONE WHO KNEW PUTIN) WERE CATAPULTED TO THE HIGHEST LEVELS OF THE GOVERNMENT AND INDUSTRY.

SERGEI CHEMEZOV, KGB COLLEAGUE

1987

SERGEI CHEMEZOV, ROSTEC CEO

2020

THEY ALL FED AT THE TROUGH AND WANTED TO OWN ACTUAL ASSETS. THEY STARTED HORNING IN ON TERRITORY THAT HAD BEEN CLAIMED BY OLIGARCHS CLOSE TO RUSSIA'S PREVIOUS PRESIDENT, BORIS YELTSIN.

MILITARY MANUFACTURING PLANT OWNED BY ROSTEC

PUTIN PUSHED YELTSIN-ERA TYCOONS OUT OF POLITICS AND CRACKED DOWN ON THOSE WHO RESISTED.

PILOT SAYS WE'RE LANDING NOW. SEE YOU SOON.

FOR EXAMPLE, IN 2003, MIKHAIL KHODORKOVSKY, RUSSIA'S RICHEST MAN, WAS ARRESTED.

GUNS ON THE TABLE! WE WILL SHOOT!

PUTIN'S MOVES ENABLED THIS FEEDING FRENZY AND THE REDISTRIBUTION OF PROPERTY OBTAINED DURING THE YELTSIN YEARS.

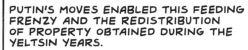

ONE OF THE THINGS THAT OUTSIDERS DON'T ALWAYS UNDERSTAND IS:

RUSSIA IS A SOCIETY THAT OPERATES ON THE BASIS OF PERSONAL TIES, NOT INSTITUTIONS OR THE RULE OF LAW.

INFORMAL UNDERSTANDINGS AND CONNECTIONS MATTER FAR MORE THAN LEGALLY BINDING CONTRACTS OR OTHER NICETIES.

IN THE ABSENCE OF TRUST, PEOPLE RELY MOST OF ALL ON FAMILY, OLD FRIENDS, OR LONGTIME ASSOCIATES.

LIKE A FEUDAL SOCIETY FROM THE MIDDLE AGES, PEOPLE PAY TRIBUTE UP THE CHAIN OF COMMAND IN EXCHANGE FOR PROTECTION.

I OFTEN THINK PART OF PUTIN'S ROLE IS TO HOLD ON TO A LITTLE BLACK NOTEBOOK...

...THAT CONTAINS A LIST OF TWO HUNDRED SIDE DEALS THAT HE'S CUT WITH THE COUNTRY'S MOST POWERFUL PLAYERS.

WHAT WE THINK OF AS CORRUPTION IS ACTUALLY THE GLUE THAT HOLDS EVERYTHING TOGETHER...

...AND MAKES THE SYSTEM SURPRISINGLY RESILIENT.

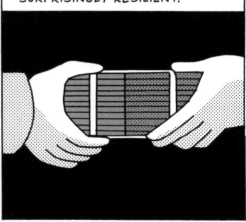

SURE, THE PEOPLE ON TOP TAKE THE BIGGEST SHARE OF THE PROCEEDS.

BUT OTHERS AT LOWER LEVELS ALSO GET A CUT.

THE ROOTS OF THIS SYSTEM RUN DEEP. DURING THE 13TH TO 15TH CENTURIES, RUS' (THE FORERUNNER OF RUSSIA) WAS CONQUERED BY THE MONGOLS AND CUT OFF FROM THE REST OF EUROPE. RUSSIAN PRINCES WERE FORCED TO BOW BEFORE THEIR ASIAN OVERLORDS AND PAY HEFTY TAXES.

IN PRE-MODERN RUSSIA, THE GRAND PRINCE OWNED THE ENTIRE COUNTRY, LITERALLY. THAT HAD A HUGELY NEGATIVE EFFECT ON ITS DEVELOPMENT.

BY CONTRAST, PRIVATE PROPERTY RIGHTS APPEARED IN ENGLAND FIVE HUNDRED YEARS BEFORE RUSSIAN NOBLES WERE ALLOWED TO OWN LAND.

RUSSIAN NOBLES CALLED THEMSELVES THE SLAVES OF THEIR RULER. IT WASN'T A TOTALLY BAD DEAL, HOWEVER.

OUT IN THE PROVINCES, THEY COULD HELP THEMSELVES TO WHATEVER WEALTH THEY COULD LAY THEIR HANDS ON.

PAY UP.

THE PROCEEDS WERE SHARED WITH NOBLEMEN FURTHER UP ON THE FOOD CHAIN.

PAY UP.

IT MADE THE EARLY RUSSIAN STATE INHERENTLY PREDATORY AND HELPED CREATE THE FOUNDATIONS OF SERFDOM, RUSSIA'S VERSION OF SLAVERY.

A REVEALING JOKE ABOUT RUSSIA: "STATE OFFICIALS ARE SACKED NOT FOR STEALING BUT FOR STEALING TOO MUCH FOR THEIR RANK."

AN APOCRYPHAL STORY STATES THAT IN THE EARLY 1800S, RUSSIA'S FAMED HISTORIAN AND MAN OF LETTERS NIKOLAI KARAMZIN HAD A CHANCE RUN-IN WITH SOME RUSSIAN ÉMIGRÉS IN FRANCE.

WE HAVEN'T BEEN HOME IN YEARS.

DID I JUST HEAR A RUSSIAN ACCENT?

WE WON'T TAKE TOO MUCH OF YOUR TIME. CAN YOU SUM UP WHAT'S GOING ON AT HOME IN A FEW WORDS?

I ONLY NEED ONE WORD.

STEALING.

THIS DEEPLY PERSONALISTIC SYSTEM AND THE CONCEPT OF TEMPORARY OWNERSHIP HAVE LARGELY SURVIVED TO THE PRESENT ERA.

THAT'S WHY ALL OF PUTIN'S ENTOURAGE AND OLIGARCHS KNOW THAT THEY ARE UNLIKELY TO HOLD ON TO THEIR PROPERTY IF HE STEPS AWAY FROM THE THRONE.

THEY ARE ALL, ESSENTIALLY, VASSALS. EXPENDABLE. NO ONE HAS AN INTEREST IN CHALLENGING THE BOSS OR GETTING ON HIS BAD SIDE.

CHAPTER

3

O LUCKY MAN!

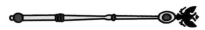

I WAS WITH PRESIDENT BILL CLINTON ON THE MORNING IN 1999 WHEN THE RUSSIANS SECRETLY TOLD HIM VLADIMIR PUTIN WAS GOING TO BE THE COUNTRY'S NEXT PRESIDENT.

OH NO! THAT GUY??

CLINTON'S TEAM WAS DUMBSTRUCK. PUTIN, A COLORLESS KGB VETERAN WITH ZERO POLITICAL EXPERIENCE, HAD BEEN PRIME MINISTER FOR ALL OF THREE WEEKS.

WOW.

JESUS.

DAMN.

HOW ON EARTH COULD SOMEONE WITH AN UNEXCEPTIONAL BACKGROUND LIKE PUTIN'S GET CATAPULTED TO SUCH AN IMPORTANT POSITION, LET ALONE TAKE OVER RUSSIA'S COLLAPSING ECONOMY AND ENORMOUS NUCLEAR ARSENAL?

THE TRUTH WAS, BORIS YELTSIN'S PRESIDENCY WAS UNRAVELING AFTER EIGHT YEARS IN POWER. HIS POPULARITY HAD HIT ROCK BOTTOM:

3–4% APPROVAL.

YELTSIN'S FAMILY AND INNER CIRCLE WERE IN PANIC MODE, FRANTICALLY LOOKING FOR A WAY TO GUARANTEE THEIR PERSONAL SECURITY, VAST WEALTH, AND STATUS IN A POST-YELTSIN RUSSIA.

YELTSIN, A NOTORIOUS BOOZEHOUND, HAD BECOME TOTALLY ERRATIC AND UNRELIABLE—WHEN HE MANAGED TO SHOW UP FOR WORK AT ALL.

IT WAS UNNERVING FOR THE WHITE HOUSE THAT THE LEADER OF A NUCLEAR SUPERPOWER WAS SERIOUSLY IMPAIRED. AT THE HEIGHT OF THE BALKANS CRISIS, HE PROPOSED A SECRET MEETING WITH CLINTON— ON A SUBMARINE.

...ON A BOAT...

YOU AND I COULD MEET WHERE NOT A SINGLE PERSON CAN DISTURB US. LIKE...

...OR SUBMARINE...

...OR ISLAND.

THE KREMLIN'S TOP-SECRET "OPERATION SUCCESSOR" KICKED INTO HIGH GEAR.

AIDES CONDUCTED POLLS, WEIGHING WHO STOOD THE BEST CHANCE OF WINNING A PRESIDENTIAL ELECTION THAT WAS LESS THAN A YEAR AWAY.

KREMLIN SPIN DOCTOR GLEB PAVLOVSKY: "WE ASKED [THEM] ABOUT MOVIE STARS..."

"...ACTORS WHO PLAYED LENIN, STALIN..."

"...PETER THE GREAT. AHEAD OF EVERYONE ELSE, QUITE UNEXPECTEDLY, WAS ANOTHER ACTOR..."

STIERLITZ!

OH! STIERLITZ.

STIERLITZ! 17 MOMENTS OF SPRING!!

"A [FICTIONAL] INTELLIGENCE OFFICER, WHO INFILTRATED THE FEARED NAZI SECRET POLICE, THE SS."

"EXCELLENTLY DRESSED, VERY WELL-MANNERED."

"IT TURNED OUT THAT PEOPLE PREFERRED HIM."

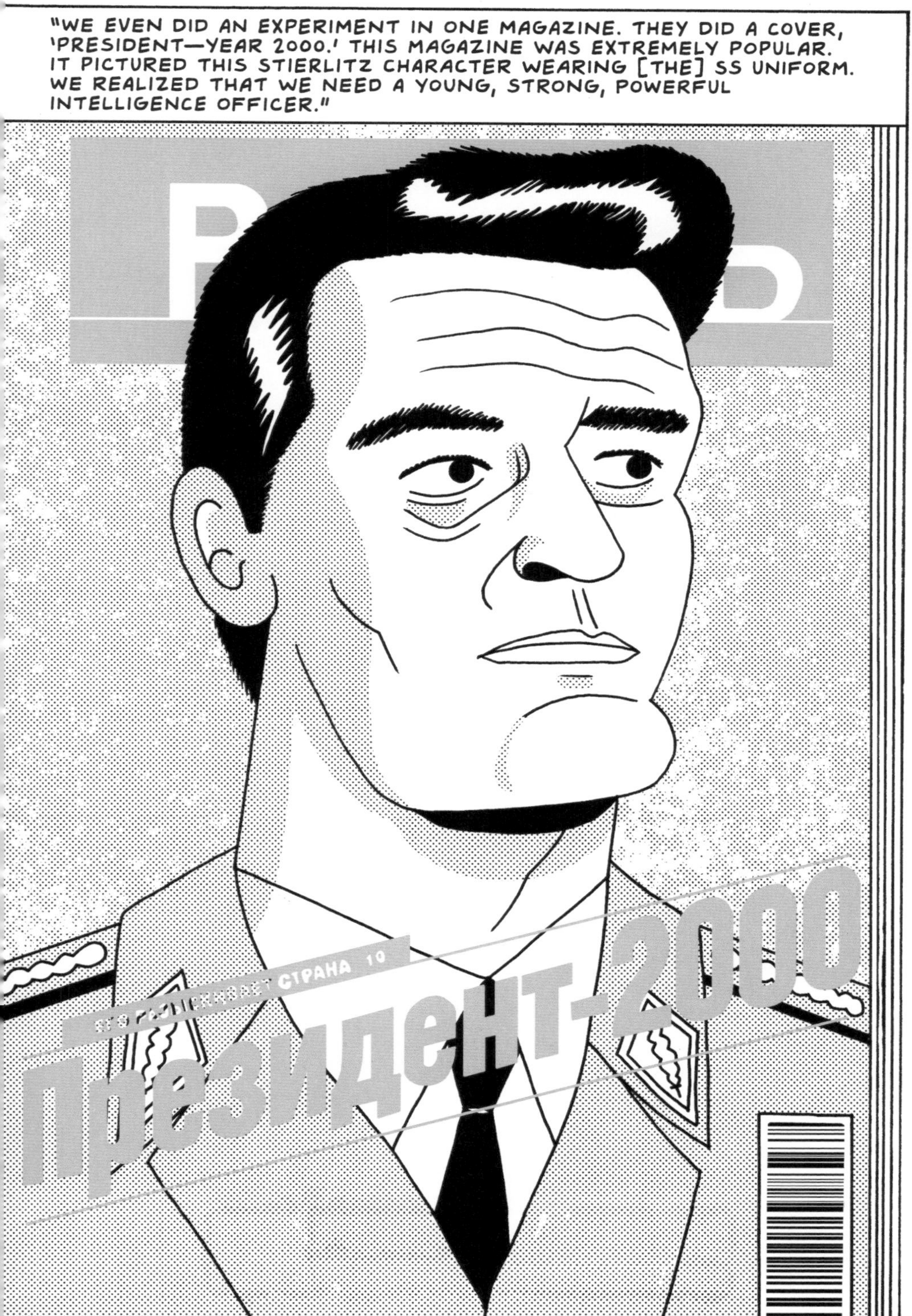
"WE EVEN DID AN EXPERIMENT IN ONE MAGAZINE. THEY DID A COVER, 'PRESIDENT—YEAR 2000.' THIS MAGAZINE WAS EXTREMELY POPULAR. IT PICTURED THIS STIERLITZ CHARACTER WEARING [THE] SS UNIFORM. WE REALIZED THAT WE NEED A YOUNG, STRONG, POWERFUL INTELLIGENCE OFFICER."
ЕГО РАЗЫСКИВАЕТ СТРАНА 10
Президент-2000

YELTSIN KEPT HIMSELF BUSY BY MAKING A BLIZZARD OF APPOINTMENTS, HIRING AND FIRING UMPTEEN PRIME MINISTERS AND SENIOR OFFICIALS.

HE STARTED SIZING UP POLITICAL TITANS AS WELL AS INTELLIGENCE AND SECURITY VETERANS WHO MIGHT PLAY TO THE PUBLIC'S AFFINITY FOR STIERLITZ.

SERGEI STEPASHIN, PRIME MINISTER, INTERIOR MINISTER

YEVGENY PRIMAKOV, PRIME MINISTER, FOREIGN MINISTER, EX-HEAD OF THE FOREIGN INTELLIGENCE SERVICE, ARABIST, RUSSIA'S VERSION OF HENRY KISSINGER.

HE'S FAMOUS FOR TURNING HIS PLANE AROUND WHEN IT WAS EN ROUTE TO WASHINGTON AT THE START OF THE KOSOVO WAR.

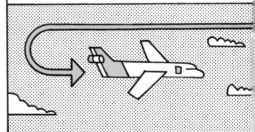

YURI LUZHKOV, THE BRASH POPULIST MAYOR OF MOSCOW, HAD TEAMED UP WITH PRIMAKOV.

THEIR NEW POLITICAL PARTY LOOKED FORMIDABLE TO YELTSIN'S TEAM.

MICHAEL JACKSON

YET INSTEAD OF PICKING SOMEONE WITH AN ESTABLISHED TRACK RECORD AND POLITICAL PROFILE, YELTSIN OPTED FOR PUTIN.

IN RUSSIAN, PUTIN WAS "Никто"—A NOBODY.

BUT IN LESS THAN TWO YEARS, HE'D ROCKETED FROM BACK OFFICE JOBS LIKE MANAGING THE KREMLIN PROPERTY OFFICE...

...AND CONDUCTING FRUITLESS INVESTIGATIONS OF CORRUPT OFFICIALS IN THE PROVINCES...

...TO TAKING OVER SOME OF THE MOST SENSITIVE POSTS IN THE KREMLIN.

HIS PAINSTAKING WORK ETHIC MADE A POSITIVE IMPRESSION.

AT THE FSB HE HAD GONE FROM BEING SOMEONE WHO BARELY MADE IT TO LIEUTENANT COLONEL...

...TO BEING BOSS OF THE ENTIRE AGENCY.

MY COLLEAGUES AT THE WHITE HOUSE AND STATE DEPARTMENT HAD A PRETTY GOOD BEAD ON PUTIN BY THIS POINT. WE'D DEALT WITH HIM ON A HANDFUL OF SENSITIVE ISSUES...

LIKE IRAN'S NUCLEAR PROGRAM...

...AND THE WAR IN THE BALKANS.

THERE WAS NO HINT OF ANY LARGER-THAN-LIFE PERSONALITY.

FORMER DEPUTY SECRETARY OF STATE STROBE TALBOTT:

HE HAS THE MANNER OF A DISCIPLINED, EFFICIENT, SELF-EFFACING EXECUTIVE ASSISTANT.

YELTSIN'S MOST IMPORTANT ADVISERS WERE HIS YOUNGER DAUGHTER TATYANA AND HER BOYFRIEND, VALENTIN YUMASHEV (WHO HAD SERVED AS KREMLIN CHIEF OF STAFF). THEY PERSUADED HIM TO PICK PUTIN.

PUTIN'S MAIN SELLING POINT WAS HIS EXCEPTIONAL LOYALTY.

WHILE WORKING IN THE KREMLIN, PUTIN HAD CHARTERED A PRIVATE JET TO SNEAK HIS FORMER BOSS ANATOLY SOBCHAK OUT OF THE COUNTRY, ONE STEP AHEAD OF A CORRUPTION INVESTIGATION.

THE YELTSIN FAMILY WAS FREAKING OUT. RUSSIA'S TOP PROSECUTOR, YURI SKURATOV, WAS HELPING HIS SWISS COUNTERPART DIG INTO THEIR DIRTY LINEN.

SUDDENLY, OUT OF NOWHERE, A GRAINY, HOUR-LONG VIDEO OF A MAN WHO LOOKED A LOT LIKE SKURATOV IN BED WITH TWO PROSTITUTES WAS SHOWN ON NATIONAL TV.

CENSORED

THEN FSB DIRECTOR PUTIN VOUCHED FOR THE TAPE AND CALLED FOR THE PROSECUTOR'S RESIGNATION. HE HELPED SAVE THE YELTSIN FAMILY'S BACON.

YELTSIN LIKED HOW PUTIN LOOKED ON TV. THE FAMILY OFFERED PUTIN A SECRET DEAL: THEY'D MAKE HIM PRESIDENT IF HE AGREED TO PROTECT YELTSIN AND HIS FAMILY.

SURE, I'M DOWN FOR WHATEVER.

EVERYONE SAW SOMETHING OF THEIR OWN IN PUTIN. LIBERALS SAW HIM AS PROVIDING CONTINUITY WITH [YELTSIN'S] IDEAS...

YUMASHEV, 2019

"...THE CHEKISTS* SAW A FORMER CHEKIST."

*THE WORD CHEKIST IS A NICKNAME FOR SOVIET/RUSSIAN INTELLIGENCE OFFICERS. THE CHEKA WAS THE NAME OF THE FIRST SOVIET INTELLIGENCE SERVICE, FOUNDED IN DECEMBER 1917.

IN A SECRETLY TAPED PRIVATE CONVERSATION, YUMASHEV'S REGRETS WERE MORE CLEAR-CUT:

WE SHOULD HAVE SPOKEN TO HIM MORE.

THE YELTSIN FAMILY WAS HOPING THEY COULD PUSH PUTIN AROUND FROM BEHIND THE SCENES.

PUTIN'S KGB PEDIGREE WAS SOMETIMES TOO CONSPICUOUS TO OVERLOOK, AS WAS THE CASE WITH MANY FORMER INTELLIGENCE OFFICERS.

HE WAS POLITE, SELF-EFFACING, AND PRECISE.

AND HE OFTEN SAID THINGS THAT HE THOUGHT YOU WANTED TO HEAR.

YES.

SOMETIMES HE'D JUST SIT THERE MUTELY, TAKING IT ALL IN AND OFFERING VERY LITTLE SUBSTANCE IN RESPONSE.

...

AT ONE OF HIS EARLIEST MEETINGS WITH THEN DEPUTY SECRETARY OF STATE STROBE TALBOTT:

I WONDER WHAT 19TH-CENTURY POET FYODOR TYUTCHEV WOULD SAY ABOUT THIS.

WHAT? FYODOR TYUTCHEV? THE SUBJECT OF MY SENIOR THESIS AT YALE?

YES. I WONDER.

AWKWARD.

COUGH

AHEM...

ALL IN THE SERVICE OF SENDING A RATHER POINTLESS MESSAGE:

SO HE READ MY KGB FILE JUST LIKE WE ASSUMED HE WOULD. BIG WHOOP.

69

IN SEPTEMBER 1999 (I.E., TWO YEARS BEFORE 9/11) PRESIDENT CLINTON'S NATIONAL SECURITY ADVISOR SANDY BERGER AND I MET PRIVATELY WITH PUTIN FOLLOWING HIS FIRST MEETING WITH CLINTON.

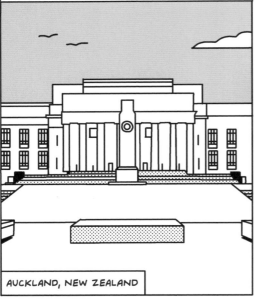

AUCKLAND, NEW ZEALAND

JUST MINUTES EARLIER, 119 PEOPLE HAD BEEN KILLED IN THE BOMBING OF A MOSCOW APARTMENT BUILDING. IT WAS THE FOURTH SUCH ATTACK IN LESS THAN TWO WEEKS.

PUTIN'S CAREER IS DOGGED TO THIS DAY BY RUMORS THAT HIS KREMLIN PATRONS OR THE FSB STAGED THE BOMBINGS TO SPEED HIS RISE TO POWER AND TO START A SMALL VICTORIOUS WAR IN CHECHNYA.

BERGER GOT RIGHT DOWN TO BUSINESS:

TERRORISM PRESENTS AN URGENT THREAT TO BOTH OF US.

RUSSIA AND THE U.S. SHOULD BE COOPERATING AGGRESSIVELY TO ELIMINATE THREATS LIKE OSAMA BIN LADEN AND AL-QAEDA.

PUTIN WAS IN COLD FISH MODE. HE DISPLAYED NO REAL INTEREST IN WORKING TOGETHER TO KILL THE WORLD'S MOST DANGEROUS TERRORIST.

SURE THING.

WHAT HE REALLY CARED ABOUT WAS THAT CHECHNYA COULD TEAR RUSSIA APART, NOT GLOBAL TERRORIST NETWORKS.

OH WELL...

A FEW DAYS LATER, THOUGH, PUTIN MADE SOME TOUGH-GUY COMMENTS ABOUT THE TERRORISTS THAT INSTANTLY ENDEARED HIM TO AVERAGE RUSSIANS.

WE'LL PURSUE THEM ANYWHERE.

EXCUSE ME FOR SAYING SO: IF WE CATCH THEM IN THE TOILET, WE'LL WIPE THEM OUT IN THE OUTHOUSE.

AND THAT'S IT, CASE CLOSED.

BUT IT WAS LARGELY AN ACT.

FORMER PUTIN ADVISOR GLEB PAVLOVSKY:

HE WAS ONE OF THOSE POLITE LENINGRAD RESIDENTS. HE COULD NOT MAKE HIMSELF SPEAK RUDELY...

...SO HE'D HAD TO BE ASKED TO ACT MORE RUDELY.

"...HE ENJOYED RIDING IN TANKS, AIRCRAFT, SUBMARINES."

"HE SHOWED THAT HE WAS YOUNG AND STRONG."

"IN THE BEGINNING, IT WAS AN IMAGE..."

"...AN IMAGE THAT ENDED UP WINNING."

EVEN TODAY PUTIN IS A PERSON "PLAYING BY MEMORY" HIS OWN IMAGE.

ONE THING WAS MOST DEFINITELY NOT AN ACT: PUTIN WAS A CARD-CARRYING *GOSUDARSTVENNIK*, A TERM THAT ELUDES EASY TRANSLATION BUT BASICALLY MEANS A SUPPORTER OF A STRONG STATE AS AN END IN ITSELF.

THE INTERESTS OF THE STATE SHOULD ALWAYS TAKE PRECEDENCE OVER THOSE OF THE INDIVIDUAL OR EVEN THE RULE OF LAW.

TO PUTIN AND OTHER *GOSUDARSTVENNIKI,* THE 1990S WERE A TOTAL HORROR SHOW. THE ECONOMY HAD BASICALLY COLLAPSED.

THE COUNTRY WAS BECOMING FRAGMENTED...

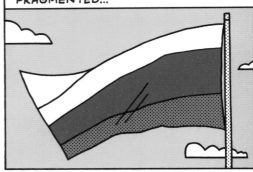

...DECENTRALIZED, AND DEINDUSTRIALIZED.

WESTERNERS CLAIMED SUCH PROBLEMS WERE MERELY THE GROWING PAINS OF A LONG-TERM TRANSITION TO A MORE DEMOCRATIC AND PROSPEROUS FUTURE.

OUR JOB WAS TO CREATE BREATHING ROOM FOR THE TRANSITION AND TO POLITELY MOLLIFY OUR RUSSIAN FRIENDS' CONCERNS.

AND, JUST AS FIRMLY, TO TELL THEM TO EAT THEIR SPINACH.

I, FOR ONE, DIDN'T APPRECIATE NEARLY ENOUGH AT THE TIME JUST HOW MUCH PUTIN'S BELIEF SYSTEM WAS DEEPLY ROOTED IN RUSSIAN HISTORY AND POLITICAL CULTURE.

FOR SOVIET AND CZARIST LEADERS ALIKE, A STRONG, CENTRALIZED STATE WAS ESSENTIAL FOR OVERSEEING A VAST, MULTIETHNIC SOCIETY.

AND FOR PROVIDING THE STRONGEST PROTECTION AGAINST HOSTILE OUTSIDE FORCES.

ACCORDING TO HISTORIAN EDWARD L. KEENAN, IT SPEAKS VOLUMES THAT EVEN "[I]N THE LATER 16TH CENTURY, WHEN THE ROUND TRIP TO THE CAPITAL COULD OCCUPY THE BETTER PART OF A YEAR, EVEN SIMPLE REAL ESTATE TRANSACTIONS CONDUCTED IN TINY VILLAGES ON THE ARCTIC CIRCLE..."

"...WERE REGISTERED AND APPROVED IN MOSCOW."

ANOTHER HISTORIAN, STEPHEN KOTKIN, HAS EXPLAINED THAT "A STRONG STATE HAS ALSO BEEN SEEN AS THE GUARANTOR OF DOMESTIC ORDER..."

"...AND THE RESULT HAS BEEN A TREND CAPTURED IN THE 19TH-CENTURY HISTORIAN VASILY KLYUCHEVSKY'S ONE-LINE SUMMATION OF A MILLENNIUM OF RUSSIAN HISTORY:"

THE STATE GREW FAT, BUT THE PEOPLE GREW LEAN.

FOR RUSSIA, GEOGRAPHY IS DESTINY. UNLIKE THE UNITED STATES, ITS BORDERS HAVE NO NATURAL DEFENSES. IT IS NOT SHIELDED BY MASSIVE OCEANS. IT CANNOT COUNT FRIENDLY COUNTRIES LIKE CANADA AND MEXICO AMONG ITS IMMEDIATE NEIGHBORS.

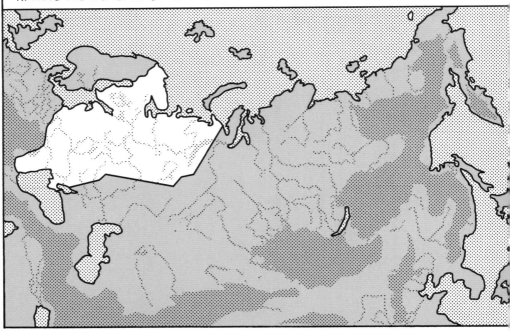

OVERRUN AT DIFFERENT POINTS IN HISTORY BY MONGOLS...

...NAPOLEON...

...AND HITLER...

...RUSSIA SAFEGUARDED ITS SECURITY THROUGH CONQUEST AND TERRITORIAL EXPANSION.

AS KOTKIN EXPLAINED, "BEGINNING WITH THE REIGN OF IVAN THE TERRIBLE IN THE 16TH CENTURY, RUSSIA MANAGED TO EXPAND AT AN AVERAGE RATE OF FIFTY SQUARE MILES PER DAY FOR HUNDREDS OF YEARS..."

"...EVENTUALLY COVERING ONE-SIXTH OF THE EARTH'S LANDMASS."

RUSSIAN TERRITORY BY 1984

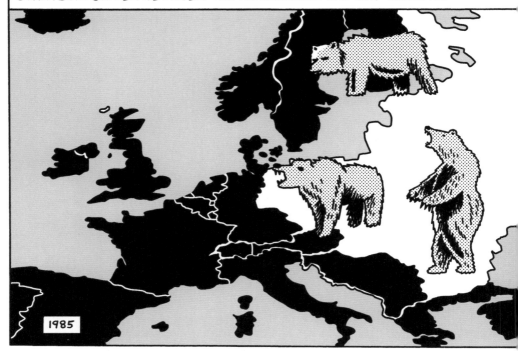

RUSSIA HAS TRADITIONALLY RELIED ON THIS EXPANDED TERRITORY AS A STRATEGIC BUFFER BETWEEN THE MOTHERLAND AND ANY THREATS.

1985

THE SHRINKING OF THAT BUFFER WHEN NATO EXPANDED IN THE 1990S AND 2000S GREATLY HEIGHTENED RUSSIAN INSECURITY.

2021

DURING PUTIN'S FIRST YEAR IN OFFICE, WE ENCOURAGED PRESIDENT CLINTON TO TEST PUTIN'S INTENTIONS AND NOT TO EMBRACE HIM PUBLICLY.

OKAY, I GOT IT!

BY WITHHOLDING THE WEST'S APPROVAL, WE FIGURED WE COULD BUY TIME FOR REFORM TO TAKE HOLD AND PERHAPS HOLD PUTIN'S FEET TO THE FIRE.

MR. PRESIDENT, REMEMBER...

CLINTON, AN UNABASHED RUSSOPHILE AND NATURAL EXTROVERT, HAD TO BE REMINDED BEFORE HIS MEETINGS WITH PUTIN:

...NO HUGGING!

I SAT IN CLINTON'S PRIVATE OFFICE IN THE RESIDENCE DURING HIS FAREWELL PHONE CHAT WITH PUTIN.

THEY'RE CONNECTING ME...

WE HAD ASKED HIM TO BRING UP RUSSIA'S BULLYING RELATIONSHIP WITH GEORGIA, A NEIGHBORING COUNTRY THAT WAS PERENNIALLY AT ODDS WITH MOSCOW.

LISTEN, MR. PRESIDENT...

YOU'RE GOING TO HAVE TO KNOCK OFF THESE PRESSURE TACTICS.

MOVE

PUTIN BASICALLY EXPLODED.

THE RAW EMOTION AND LACK OF SELF-CONTROL FROM A HEAD OF STATE WERE THINGS I HADN'T SEEN BEFORE.

PUTIN GOT MORE AND MORE HEATED...

...ESPECIALLY COMPARED TO THE SMOOTH-AS-SILK CLINTON.

IT WAS SCARY TO SEE PUTIN ACTING LIKE A TOTAL HOTHEAD.

BEFORE TOO LONG, THE IMPULSIVE STREAK THAT HAD HURT HIS KGB CAREER WOULD BEGIN TO STIR TROUBLE ON A MUCH VASTER SCALE.

CHAPTER
4

INTO THE ABYSS

FOR A SEEMINGLY OMNIPOTENT FIGURE...

...VLADIMIR PUTIN WEARS HIS INSECURITIES ON HIS SLEEVE.

THE KREMLIN'S WORLDVIEW WAS CRYSTALLIZED IN THE EARLY 2000S. NONVIOLENT STREET PROTESTS—DUBBED "COLOR REVOLUTIONS"— BROUGHT DOWN A SERIES OF HATED LEADERS.

FOR EXAMPLE, IN 2000, A SCRAGGLY GROUP OF SERBIAN STUDENTS AND POLITICAL ACTIVISTS LED A MOVEMENT...

...TO OVERTHROW LEADER SLOBODAN MILOŠEVIĆ, WHOM THE RUSSIANS WERE FRIENDLY WITH.

U.S.-FUNDED EXPERTS TAUGHT THE SERBS HOW TO STAGE A REVOLUTION USING NONVIOLENT STREET PROTESTS.

THEY RELIED ON THE TEACHINGS OF A SEVENTY-SOMETHING U.S. COLLEGE PROFESSOR NAMED GENE SHARP...

...WHOSE LIFE'S WORK WAS ALL ABOUT FIGURING OUT WAYS TO TOPPLE DICTATORS.

SHARP DEVELOPED A
PLAYBOOK OF 198
METHODS OF NON-
VIOLENT ACTION.
AMONG THEM:

The Politics of
Nonviolent
Action

PART 2

THE

METHODS OF
NONVIOLENT
ACTION

GENE SHARP

DISPLAYS AND FLAGS
AND SYMBOLIC COLORS

HUMOROUS SKITS AND
PRANKS

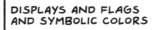

PACK YOUR
BAGS, PAL!

PROTEST DISROBINGS

STOP
FEMICIDE

RUDE GESTURES

DESTRUCTION OF OWN
PROPERTY

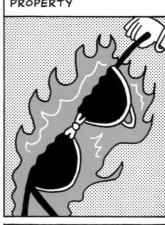

SKYWRITING AND
EARTHWRITING

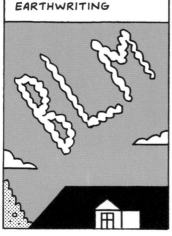

MOCK FUNERALS

DISPLAY OF PORTRAITS

WHO
IS TO
BLAME?

SERBIAN ACTIVISTS EVEN RAN ANTI-MILOŠEVIĆ TV ADS.

BELIEVE ME, I'VE TRIED EVERYTHING.

IT WON'T COME CLEAN.

BUT THIS HAS A SPECIAL SETTING.

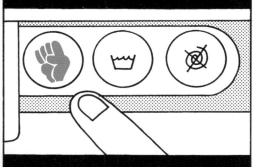

IT'LL CLEAN THIS AND OTHER SIMILAR STAINS.

SEE, IT WORKS!

THE U.S. PAID FOR FIVE THOUSAND CANS OF SPRAY PAINT...

...AS WELL AS 2.5 MILLION BUMPER STICKERS WITH STUDENT MOVEMENT OTPOR'S FIST LOGO...

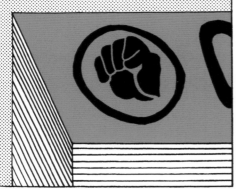

...AND THE SLOGAN "GOTOV JE," WHICH MEANS "HE'S FINISHED."

THEY BECAME UBIQUITOUS SYMBOLS.

DICTATORS ARE NEVER AS STRONG AS THEY TELL YOU THEY ARE, AND PEOPLE ARE NEVER AS WEAK AS THEY THINK THEY ARE.

"THE EXTREME REPRESSION COMES WHEN A DICTATORSHIP REALLY IS FRIGHTENED..."

"...AND THEREFORE THEY ACT RUTHLESSLY."

SHARP FIGURED OUT THAT THIS IS ALSO PRECISELY THE MOMENT WHEN A REGIME CAN BE MOST EASILY BROKEN APART.

LIKE PUTIN, SHARP EMBRACED MARTIAL ARTS METAPHORS:

"POLITICAL JIU-JITSU IS A PROCESS BY WHICH NONVIOLENT ACTION DEALS WITH VIOLENT REPRESSION..."

"...AND CAUSES THE ADVERSARIES' REPRESSION TO BE EXPOSED IN THE WORST POSSIBLE LIGHT."

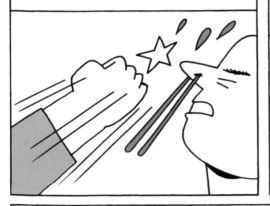

"THIS, IN TURN, MAY LEAD TO SHIFTS IN OPINION..."

FOUL!

"...AND THEN TO SHIFTS IN POWER RELATIONSHIPS FAVORABLE TO THE NONVIOLENT GROUP."

I WAS NOT A MEMBER OF THE CIA. I NEVER HAVE BEEN. NEVER WILL BE. AND IF YOU DON'T BELIEVE ME...

...GO F**K YOURSELF!

ROBERT HELVEY, A RETIRED U.S. ARMY COLONEL AND ONE OF SHARP'S DISCIPLES, HELPED LEAD THE TRAINING OF ACTIVISTS.

ALL OF THE PREPARATIONS BEING MADE IN SERBIA AND NEARBY HUNGARY BY SERBIAN ACTIVISTS WERE NO LAUGHING MATTER FOR THE KREMLIN. MAYBE THAT'S BECAUSE THEY HAD AN INKLING ABOUT THE MILLIONS OF DOLLARS THE CIA HAD SECRETLY SPENT TO FINANCE THE SERBIAN OPPOSITION.

LIVE

CNN MILOSEVIC OUSTED

BILL CLINTON AUTHORIZED THE COVERT OPERATION.

I DIDN'T HAVE A PROBLEM WITH IT.

BECAUSE MILOŠEVIĆ "WAS A STONE-COLD KILLER AND HAD CAUSED THE DEATHS OF HUNDREDS OF THOUSANDS OF PEOPLE..."

BRAKKA BRAKKA BRAKKA

BRAKKA BRAKKA BRAKKA

WE DID NOT RIG THE VOTE NOR KNOWINGLY LIE TO THE VOTERS TO GET THEM TO SUPPORT THE PEOPLE WE HOPED TO WIN.

THERE'S A DEATH THRESHOLD...

...AND MILOŠEVIĆ CROSSED IT.

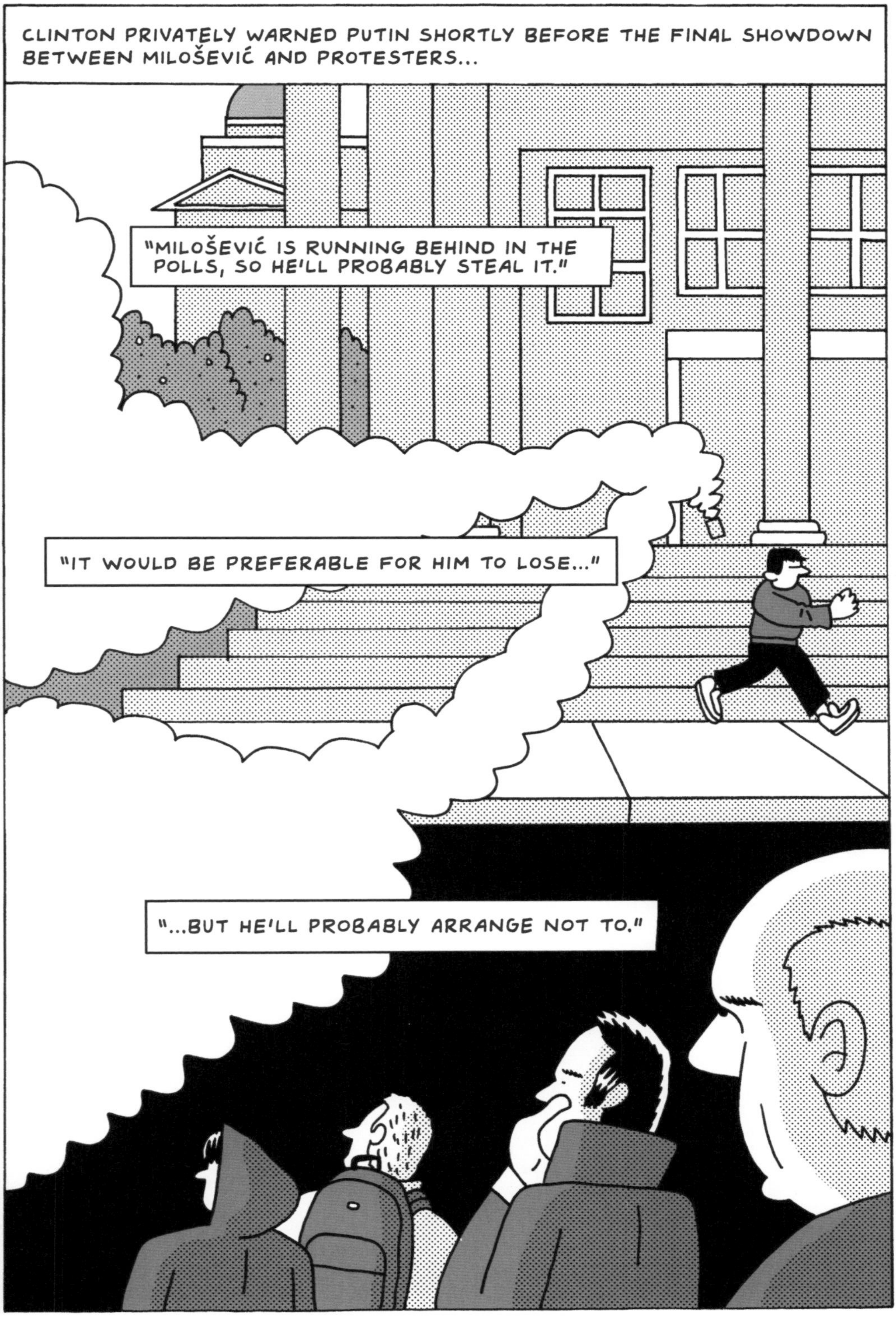
CLINTON PRIVATELY WARNED PUTIN SHORTLY BEFORE THE FINAL SHOWDOWN BETWEEN MILOŠEVIĆ AND PROTESTERS...
"MILOŠEVIĆ IS RUNNING BEHIND IN THE POLLS, SO HE'LL PROBABLY STEAL IT."
"IT WOULD BE PREFERABLE FOR HIM TO LOSE..."
"...BUT HE'LL PROBABLY ARRANGE NOT TO."

MILOŠEVIĆ GOT CREAMED IN THE ELECTION AND THEN CLUMSILY TRIED TO RIG IT...

...FALLING INTO THE TRAP SET BY THE CLINTON TEAM AND GENE SHARP'S ACOLYTES.

BEFORE TOO LONG, HE WAS SWEPT FROM POWER.

SEVERAL YEARS LATER, HE WAS TRIED FOR WAR CRIMES IN THE HAGUE.

HE DIED IN A PRISON CELL.

AFTER MILOŠEVIĆ'S OUSTER, THE KREMLIN WAS RATTLED BY A WAVE OF COLOR REVOLUTIONS ACROSS THE FORMER SOVIET UNION. THOSE UPRISINGS INCLUDING GEORGIA'S ROSE REVOLUTION (2003) AND KYRGYZSTAN'S TULIP REVOLUTION (2005).

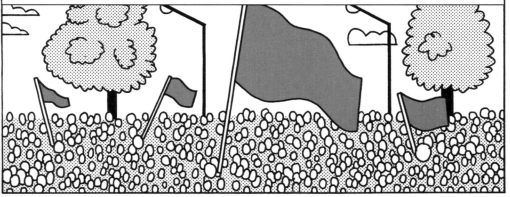

HEAVY-HANDED KREMLIN MEDDLING IN UKRAINE'S 2004 PRESIDENTIAL ELECTION INADVERTENTLY SET IN MOTION THE ORANGE REVOLUTION...

...ONE OF THE MOST HUMILIATING MOMENTS OF PUTIN'S PRESIDENCY.

IN MAY 2004, THEN-PRESIDENT BUSH'S NATIONAL SECURITY ADVISER CONDOLEEZZA RICE VISITED PUTIN AT HIS RESIDENCE OUTSIDE MOSCOW. HE HAD A SURPRISE IN STORE FOR HER.

MEET VIKTOR YANUKOVYCH, WHO IS RUNNING FOR THE PRESIDENCY OF UKRAINE.

ACCORDING TO RICE, "YANUKOVYCH SUDDENLY APPEARED FROM A BACK ROOM."

"PUTIN WANTED ME TO GET THE POINT. HE'S MY MAN, UKRAINE IS OURS—AND DON'T FORGET IT."

PUTIN SHOWED UP IN KYIV ON THE EVE OF THE ELECTION.

RUSSIAN SPIN DOCTORS AND CAMPAIGN STRATEGISTS WERE ON HAND, TOO.

THEY THOUGHT THEY WERE HELPING ENGINEER VIKTOR YANUKOVYCH'S VICTORY OVER A FORMER BANKER...

...NAMED VIKTOR YUSHCHENKO, WHO HAD MOBILIZED WESTERN-ORIENTED AND NATIONALIST FORCES.

YUSHCHENKO WAS POISONED WITH DIOXIN ON THE EVE OF THE VOTE.

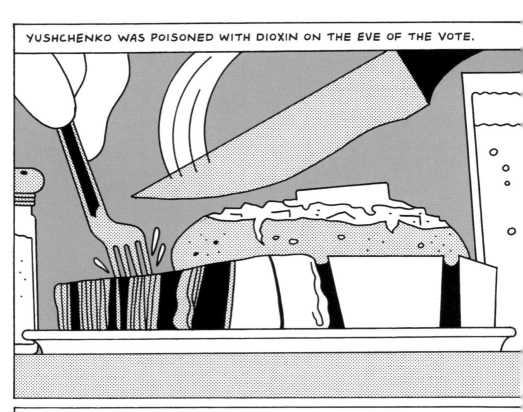

HE SURVIVED, BARELY, BUT HIS ONCE HANDSOME FACE WAS PERMANENTLY SCARRED.

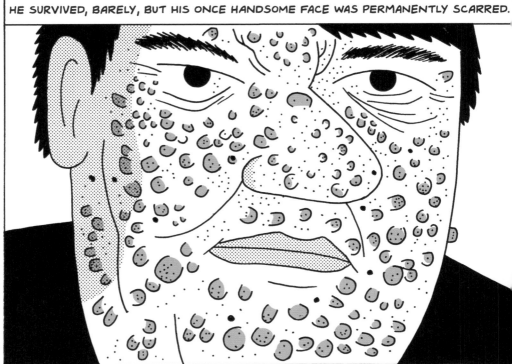

YUSCHENKO'S SUPPORTERS, ONE MILLION STRONG, TOOK TO THE STREETS UNDER ORANGE BANNERS AFTER THE ELECTION WAS BLATANTLY STOLEN.

EVENTUALLY YANUKOVYCH AGREED TO RERUN THE VOTE, WHICH HE LOST.

I HAD A CONTRACT FROM THE KREMLIN TO WIN THE ELECTION FOR YANUKOVYCH...

GLEB PAVLOVSKY, KREMLIN POLITICAL ADVISER

...WHICH I DID...

"BUT WE WERE FACED WITH A REVOLUTION..."

AND I HAD NO CONTRACT TO STOP THAT.

IT WAS A GRASSROOTS REVOLUTION, BUT PUTIN SAW U.S. FINGERPRINTS ALL OVER IT.

THE STATE DEPARTMENT AND USAID HAD FUNDED UKRAINIAN CIVIL SOCIETY AND ACTIVIST GROUPS.

U.S.-TRAINED ACTIVISTS FROM SERBIA AND A HOST OF U.S. PRO-DEMOCRACY NGOS SHOWED UP, TOO...

AS DID THE U.S. FOUNDATION LED BY BILLIONAIRE PHILANTHROPIST GEORGE SOROS...

...ONE OF PUTIN'S PERENNIAL NEMESES.

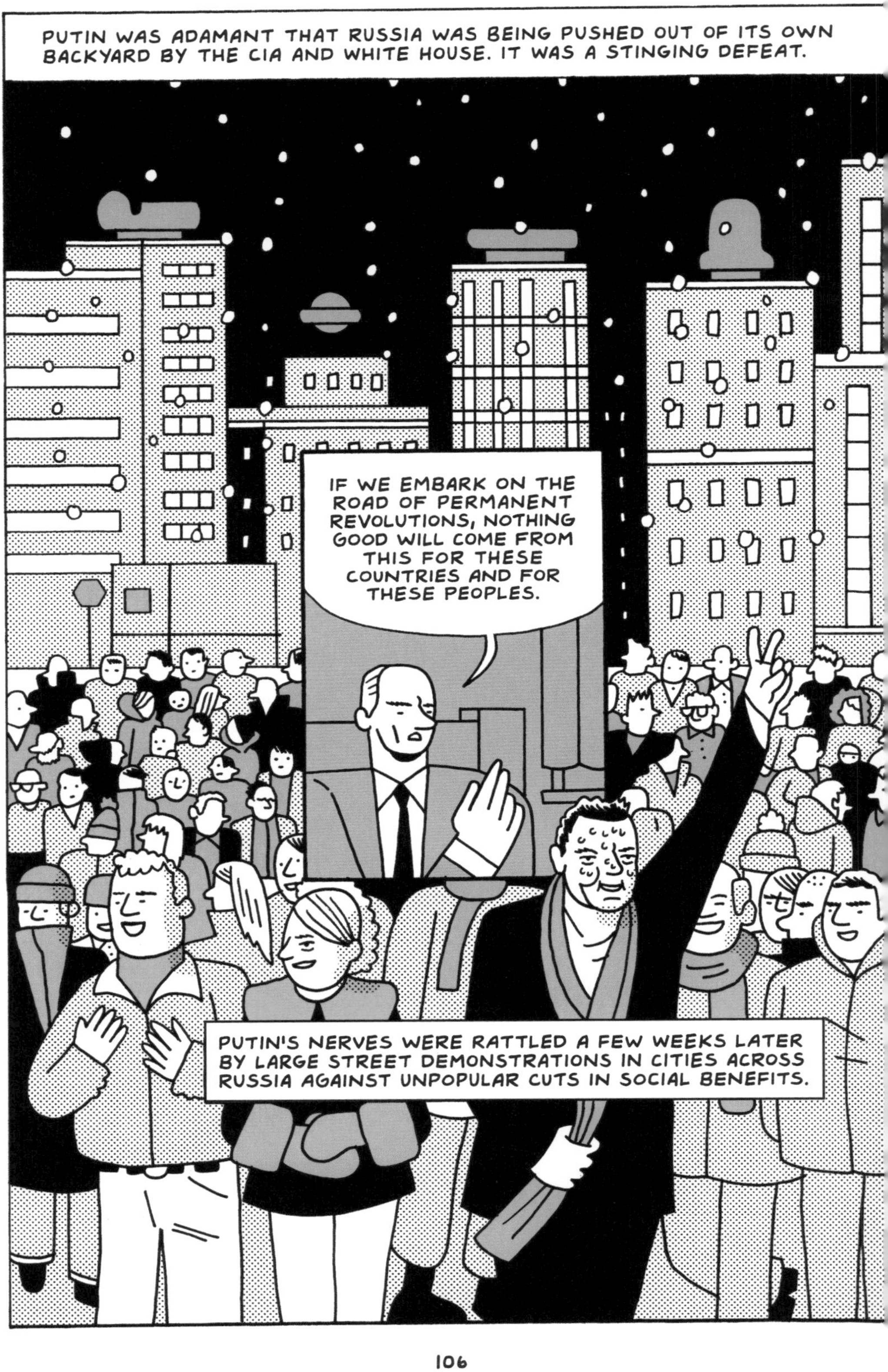
PUTIN WAS ADAMANT THAT RUSSIA WAS BEING PUSHED OUT OF ITS OWN BACKYARD BY THE CIA AND WHITE HOUSE. IT WAS A STINGING DEFEAT.
IF WE EMBARK ON THE ROAD OF PERMANENT REVOLUTIONS, NOTHING GOOD WILL COME FROM THIS FOR THESE COUNTRIES AND FOR THESE PEOPLES.
PUTIN'S NERVES WERE RATTLED A FEW WEEKS LATER BY LARGE STREET DEMONSTRATIONS IN CITIES ACROSS RUSSIA AGAINST UNPOPULAR CUTS IN SOCIAL BENEFITS.

THE KREMLIN'S SETBACKS IN UKRAINE WERE MORE THAN A POLITICAL BLACK EYE.

TO PUTIN'S INNER CIRCLE, THEY LOOKED LIKE A DRESS REHEARSAL...

...FOR A WESTERN ONSLAUGHT ON THE RUSSIAN REGIME.

PRIOR TO THE ORANGE REVOLUTION, PUTIN HAD ALREADY BEEN ON EDGE: JUST A COUPLE MONTHS EARLIER IN SEPTEMBER 2004, CHECHEN MILITANTS HAD TAKEN MORE THAN 1,200 CHILDREN AND ADULTS HOSTAGE...

...ON THE FIRST DAY OF SCHOOL IN A SMALL TOWN NAMED BESLAN.

AFTER A THREE-DAY SIEGE, A BOTCHED RESCUE OPERATION ENDED IN CHAOS AND BLOODSHED.

MORE THAN THREE HUNDRED CHILDREN AND ADULTS DIED DURING TEN HOURS OF FIGHTING.

THE CARNAGE WAS BROADCAST LIVE WORLDWIDE.

CNN SCHOOL SIEGE 11:04

THE ACCOUNTS OF HUMAN SUFFERING AND TERROR WERE HORRIFIC.

THE TERRORISTS PREVENTED THE HOSTAGES FROM USING THE BATHROOM AND DENIED THEM WATER.

KIDS DRANK THEIR OWN URINE.

THE ATTACK WAS AS TRAUMATIC FOR MANY RUSSIANS AS 9/11 WAS FOR AMERICANS.

MORE THAN FIFTEEN YEARS LATER, IT'S STILL AN OPEN WOUND.

THE ROOT CAUSES OF THE CHECHEN CONFLICT STRETCH BACK TO THE 1700S, WHEN PETER THE GREAT AND CATHERINE THE GREAT PUSHED INTO THE REGION.

FIERCE CHECHEN WARRIORS ON HORSEBACK FREQUENTLY RAIDED RUSSIAN VILLAGES...

...AT THE FOOT OF THE CAUCASUS MOUNTAINS, THE TALLEST RANGE IN EUROPE.

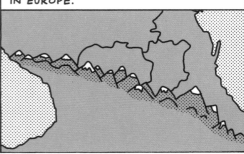

THEY MADE OFF WITH CATTLE, HORSES, AND HOSTAGES.

THE CZARIST ARMY'S BRUTAL CAMPAIGN IN CHECHNYA IN THE MID-1800S WAS CHRONICLED BY LEO TOLSTOY, WHO SPENT THREE YEARS IN THE REGION.

OFFICER TOLSTOY

TOLSTOY WAS DISGUSTED BY THE WAR YET ENCHANTED BY THE CHECHENS' MARTIAL CULTURE AND RESISTANCE TO AUTHORITY.

NO ONE SPOKE OF HATRED FOR THE RUSSIANS.

THE FEELING THAT ALL CHECHENS FELT, BOTH YOUNG AND OLD, WAS STRONGER THAN HATRED...

...A REFUSAL TO RECOGNIZE THESE RUSSIAN DOGS AS PEOPLE.

DURING WWII, STALIN DEPORTED THE ENTIRE CHECHEN POPULATION IN CATTLE CARS AND DUMPED THEM IN THE MIDDLE OF NOWHERE IN KAZAKHSTAN, ONE THOUSAND MILES AWAY.

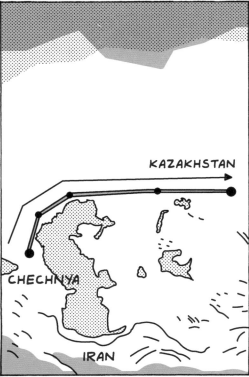

MORE THAN ONE IN FIVE OF THE DEPORTEES DIED. STALIN'S SECRET POLICE MASSACRED SOME OLD AND SICK CHECHENS INSTEAD OF TRANSPORTING THEM.

THEN, IN THE 1990S, YELTSIN WAGED A DISASTROUS WAR IN CHECHNYA THAT KILLED TENS OF THOUSANDS AND LEFT THE REGION QUASI-INDEPENDENT FROM MOSCOW.

STUNG BY CRITICISM OVER THE BESLAN DEBACLE, PUTIN BECAME CONVINCED THE U.S. WAS SECRETLY SUPPORTING CHECHEN INDEPENDENCE.

IN HIS TELLING, PRESIDENT BUSH WAS A HYPOCRITE. PUTIN'S FIGHT IN CHECHNYA WAS NO DIFFERENT THAN AMERICA'S WAR ON TERROR.

IMMEDIATELY AFTER 9/11, BUSH FAMOUSLY WARNED:

EVERY NATION, IN EVERY REGION, NOW HAS A DECISION TO MAKE. EITHER YOU ARE WITH US OR YOU ARE WITH THE TERRORISTS.

PUTIN BELIEVED THAT THE U.S. WAS SUPPORTING THE CHECHEN CAUSE AS A WAY TO PUT PRESSURE ON HIM.

WHEN PUTIN SPOKE TO A GRIEVING NATION ABOUT BESLAN, HE SHIFTED BLAME FOR THE ATTACK TO THE U.S., CLAIMING THAT PRESIDENT BUSH WAS TRYING TO DISMEMBER RUSSIA.

SOME WANT TO TEAR OFF OF US A JUICY MORSEL.

OTHERS HELP THEM DO IT.

THEY HELP BECAUSE THEY THINK THAT RUSSIA, AS ONE OF THE GREATEST NUCLEAR POWERS OF THE WORLD, IS STILL A THREAT...

...AND THIS THREAT HAS TO BE ELIMINATED.

AND TERRORISM IS ONLY AN INSTRUMENT TO ACHIEVE THESE GOALS.

A 2006 REPORT BY A RUSSIAN PARLIAMENTARY COMMISSION INTO THE BESLAN ATTACK WHITEWASHED THE GOVERNMENT'S MISTAKES.

THE COMMISSION WAS LED BY A FORMER PROSECUTOR, ALEKSANDR TORSHIN...

...WHO WOULD RESURFACE IN 2016 AS ONE OF THE RUSSIAN GOVERNMENT'S CONDUITS TO DONALD J. TRUMP'S PRESIDENTIAL CAMPAIGN TEAM AND PRO-GOP CONSERVATIVE GROUPS LIKE THE NATIONAL RIFLE ASSOCIATION.

IN THE WAKE OF THESE BACK-TO-BACK BLOWS FROM CHECHEN TERRORISM AND THE ORANGE REVOLUTION IN UKRAINE...

...THE KREMLIN BECAME OBSESSED WITH PROTECTING ITSELF FROM U.S. PRESSURE CAMPAIGNS.

IN 2007, PUTIN PULLED ASIDE THE U.S. AMBASSADOR AND ISSUED A CHILLING WARNING:

OUTSIDE INTERFERENCE IN OUR ELECTIONS WILL NOT BE TOLERATED.

WE KNOW YOU HAVE DIPLOMATS...

...AND PEOPLE WHO PRETEND TO BE DIPLOMATS...

...TRAVELING ALL OVER RUSSIA ENCOURAGING OPPOSITIONISTS.

DON'T THINK WE WON'T REACT TO OUTSIDE INTERFERENCE.

TO PUTIN, STREET PROTESTS, NGOS, AND PEOPLE POWER LOOKED LIKE SERIOUS SECURITY THREATS.

THE KREMLIN ORGANIZED A MILITANT YOUTH MOVEMENT NAMED *NASHI* (OURS)...

...DECKED OUT WITH GENE SHARP—QUALITY LOGOS...

...MATCHING TRACKSUITS...

...AND FLAGS.

THEY WERE TRAINED TO DEFEAT SUBVERSIVES THAT PUTIN'S TEAM BELIEVED WERE BEING PAID BY WASHINGTON TO ORGANIZE STREET PROTESTS.

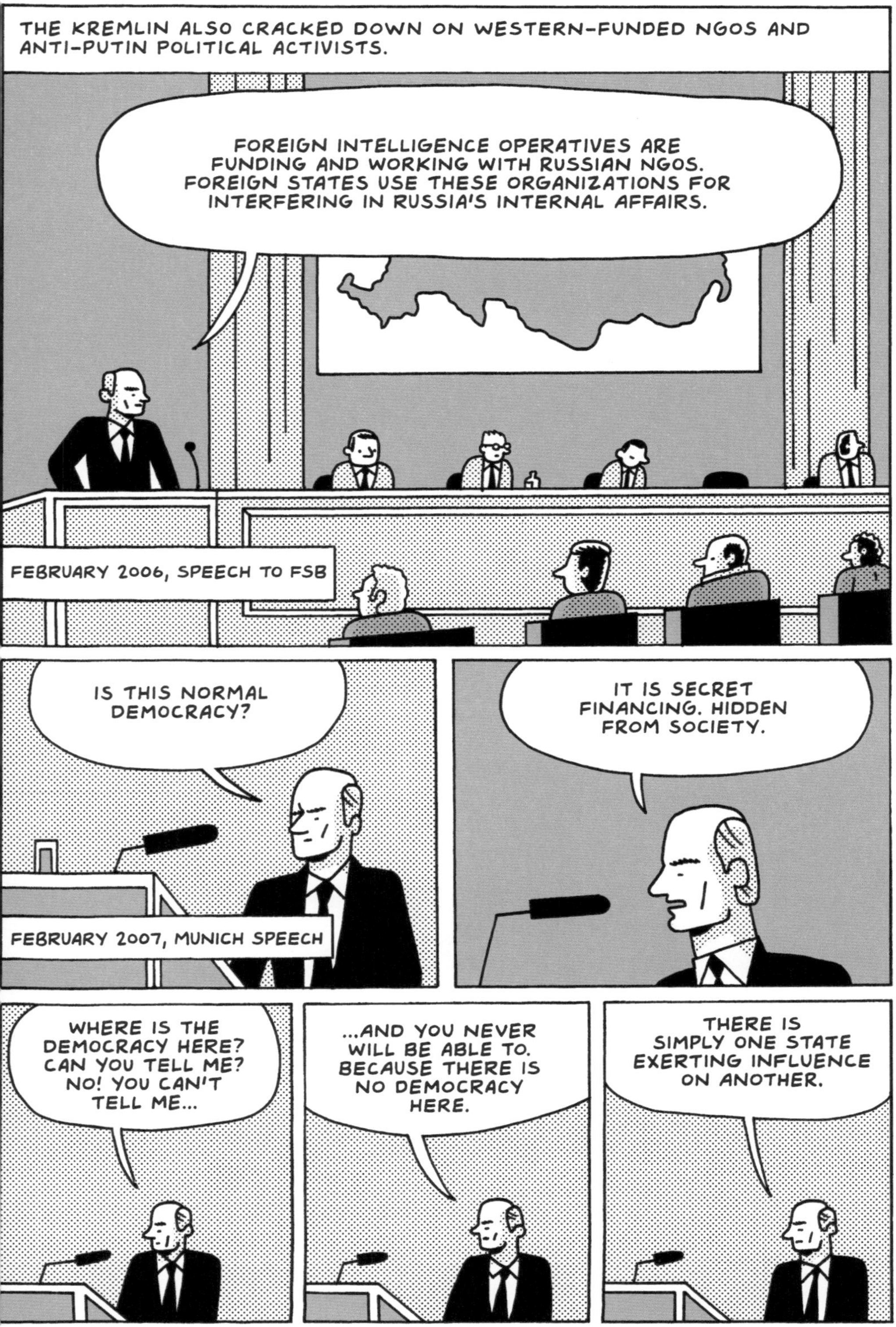
THE KREMLIN ALSO CRACKED DOWN ON WESTERN-FUNDED NGOS AND ANTI-PUTIN POLITICAL ACTIVISTS.
FOREIGN INTELLIGENCE OPERATIVES ARE FUNDING AND WORKING WITH RUSSIAN NGOS. FOREIGN STATES USE THESE ORGANIZATIONS FOR INTERFERING IN RUSSIA'S INTERNAL AFFAIRS.
FEBRUARY 2006, SPEECH TO FSB
IS THIS NORMAL DEMOCRACY?
FEBRUARY 2007, MUNICH SPEECH
IT IS SECRET FINANCING. HIDDEN FROM SOCIETY.
WHERE IS THE DEMOCRACY HERE? CAN YOU TELL ME? NO! YOU CAN'T TELL ME...
...AND YOU NEVER WILL BE ABLE TO. BECAUSE THERE IS NO DEMOCRACY HERE.
THERE IS SIMPLY ONE STATE EXERTING INFLUENCE ON ANOTHER.

ALTHOUGH PUTIN'S APPROVAL RATINGS HAVE BARELY EVER DIPPED BELOW 60% FOR HIS ENTIRE TIME IN POWER...

...HE IS CERTAIN ALL OPPOSITION GROUPS ARE THE HANDIWORK OF FOREIGN ENEMIES SEEKING A COLOR REVOLUTION.

IN PUTIN'S CONSPIRACY-INFUSED VIEW OF THE WORLD, AMERICA'S DIPLOMATS, INTELLIGENCE SERVICES, NGOS, AND TECHNOLOGY COMPANIES WORK HAND IN HAND TO ORGANIZE STREET PROTESTS TO GET RID OF GOVERNMENTS THE U.S. DOESN'T LIKE.

PEOPLE POWER IS NEVER HOMEGROWN. IT IS A CLEAR AND PRESENT DANGER.

KA-THUD

THE INTERNET? FOR PUTIN, IT'S A "CIA PROJECT."

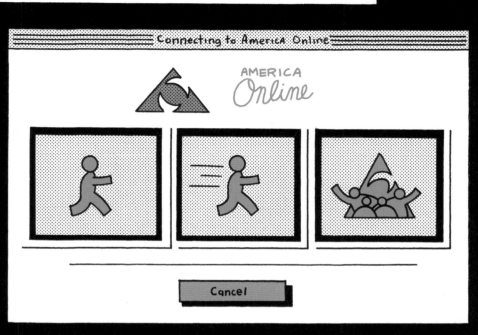

ALL OF THIS IS A CLASSIC CASE OF MIRROR IMAGING.

WEE-WAAAAAA

SINCE RUSSIA OPERATES THIS WAY, SURELY ITS MAIN ADVERSARY MUST DO THE SAME THING.

THERE WAS A WHOLE SERIES OF CONTROLLED "COLOR" REVOLUTIONS.

CLEARLY, THE PEOPLE IN THOSE NATIONS, WHERE THESE EVENTS TOOK PLACE, WERE SICK OF TYRANNY...

"...AND POVERTY, OF THEIR LACK OF PROSPECTS..."

...BUT THESE FEELINGS WERE TAKEN ADVANTAGE OF CYNICALLY [BY THE WEST].

WHEN THE ARAB SPRING ERUPTED IN LATE 2011, THE RUSSIAN LEADERSHIP WAS CONVINCED WASHINGTON WAS BEHIND IT.

PUTIN MISTAKENLY THINKS THAT THERE IS A "COLOR REVOLUTION" BUTTON ON THE DESK OF THE U.S. PRESIDENT.

RUSSIAN LEADERS SIMPLY CAN'T ACCEPT THAT BRAVE PEOPLE SOMETIMES SHAPE HISTORY ALL ON THEIR OWN.

WE UNDERSTAND WHAT IS HAPPENING.

LOOK WHAT THEY HAVE DONE IN EGYPT...

IGOR SECHIN, ONE OF PUTIN'S CLOSEST ASSOCIATES

"...THOSE HIGHLY PLACED MANAGERS OF GOOGLE..."

"...WHAT MANIPULATIONS OF THE ENERGY OF THE PEOPLE TOOK PLACE THERE."

WE WANT INTERNET

ALL "COLOR REVOLUTIONS" HAVE A SIMILAR PATTERN...

NIKOLAI PATRUSHEV, PUTIN'S NATIONAL SECURITY ADVISER AND FORMER FSB DIRECTOR

"THE WEST GIVES INFORMATION AND MATERIAL SUPPORT TO PROTEST ACTIVITY..."

"...APPLAUDS THE VIOLENT OVERTHROW OF THE CURRENT GOVERNMENT..."

"...THEN BRINGS ITS PUPPETS TO POWER."

THE WEST HAS DEVELOPED A POWERFUL ARSENAL OF INTERFERENCE IN THE INTERNAL AFFAIRS OF SOVEREIGN STATES THAT POSES A SERIOUS THREAT TO INTERNATIONAL SECURITY.

GIVEN HOW QUICKLY THE RUSSIAN STATE COLLAPSED TWICE IN THE 20TH CENTURY...

...IT DOESN'T SEEM TOTALLY OUT OF LINE FOR PUTIN TO BE WORRIED ABOUT THIS KIND OF THING.

INSIDE THE KREMLIN, THESE ATTITUDES HAVE FOSTERED A PERMANENT STATE OF SIEGE.

PUTIN AND HIS POLITICAL GURUS DECIDED LONG AGO THAT RUSSIA CAN'T HAVE REAL POLITICAL COMPETITION...

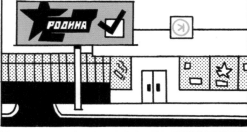

...OR A TOTALLY FREE INTERNET...

...OR TOTALLY FREE MEDIA BECAUSE, WELL, YOU NEVER KNOW. THINGS MIGHT JUST GET OUT OF HAND.

RUSSIA'S RESTRICTIONS ON POLITICAL ACTIVITY SOMETIMES SMACK OF THE ABSURD. THE FORMER SPEAKER OF THE STATE DUMA, RUSSIA'S VERSION OF PARLIAMENT, WAS LAMPOONED FOR CLAIMING:

AHEM...

...THE DUMA IS NOT A PLACE FOR DISCUSSION.

EVEN THE TOKEN OPPOSITION PARTIES ALLOWED TO SIT IN PARLIAMENT (E.G., THE COMMUNISTS) ARE TOTALLY UNDER THE THUMB OF THE KREMLIN.

IN PUTIN'S VIEW, THREATS OF FOREIGN INTERFERENCE ARE EXISTENTIAL, NOT THEORETICAL. RUSSIA'S VERY SURVIVAL AS A SOVEREIGN NATION IS AT STAKE.

THAT'S A BIG PART OF THE REASON WHY PUTIN AND OTHER LEADERS, LIKE CHINA'S XI JINPING, FEEL A NATURAL AFFINITY FOR EACH OTHER AND EXHIBIT SO MUCH WARINESS ABOUT U.S. INTENTIONS.

THEY HUNGER FOR GREATER CONTROL OVER THEIR CITIZENS' LIVES. THEY IMPOSE LIMITS ON ACCESS TO INFORMATION AND THE INTERNET, WHICH THEY SEE AS VEHICLES FOR WESTERN INFLUENCE.

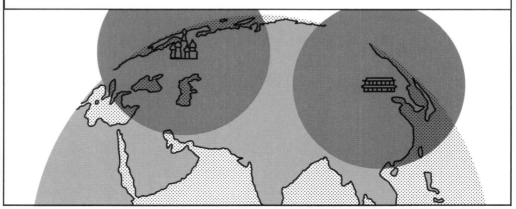

GIVEN ALL THIS, IT'S EASY TO SEE WHY ANY SPONTANEOUS STREET PROTEST LOOKS SO THREATENING TO PUTIN.

TO HIM, THE LEADERS OF SUCH PROTESTS ARE USUALLY FOREIGN-BACKED PROVOCATEURS, JUST LIKE LENIN AND THE BOLSHEVIKS WERE.

WE HAVE SUCH PEOPLE IN OUR NATION TODAY AS WELL.

THE KREMLIN IS ADAMANT: DEMANDS FOR POLITICAL CHANGE ARE ALWAYS THE RESULT OF WESTERN-BACKED CONSPIRACIES.

МИР ЗЕМЛЯ ХЛЕБ

PETROGRAD, OCTOBER 1917

PEACE LAND BREAD (МИР ЗЕМЛЯ ХЛЕБ)—BOLSHEVIK REVOLUTIONARY SLOGAN

ACCORDING TO THE HEAD OF THE RUSSIAN HISTORICAL SOCIETY, SERGEI NARYSHKIN...

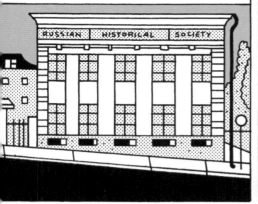

...WHO JUST SO HAPPENS TO ALSO BE THE HEAD OF RUSSIA'S FOREIGN INTELLIGENCE SERVICE (YOU REALLY CAN'T MAKE THIS STUFF UP)...

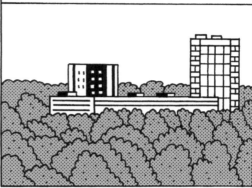

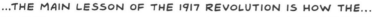

...THE MAIN LESSON OF THE 1917 REVOLUTION IS HOW THE...

IMPORT OF SO-CALLED REVOLUTIONARY KNOW-HOW AND COLOR REVOLUTIONS...

ALWAYS BRING WITH THEM BLOOD, THE DEATH OF CITIZENS, DESTRUCTION, AND CALAMITIES FOR THE COUNTRIES THAT FALL VICTIM TO SUCH AN EXPERIMENT.

WHAT'S PARAMOUNT FOR RUSSIA, NARYSHKIN INSISTS, IS PRESERVING STABILITY IN THE FACE OF...

THOSE CENTERS, PRIMARILY BEYOND THE OCEAN...

...WHERE THE DECISIONS TO FUND COUPS D'ÉTAT ARE MADE.

PUTIN STRONGLY OPPOSES ANY LOOSENING UP OF RUSSIA'S POLITICS AND ECONOMY BECAUSE HE FEARS INSTABILITY.

YES, SIR.

AS A YOUNG KGB OFFICER IN EAST GERMANY IN LATE 1989, PUTIN WITNESSED WHAT HAPPENS WHEN PEOPLE RISE UP AND CHALLENGE AN UNPOPULAR REGIME.

YES, SIR.

LATE THAT YEAR, THOUSANDS OF PRO-DEMOCRACY PROTESTERS IN DRESDEN TOOK OVER THE HEADQUARTERS OF THE SECRET POLICE.

WE ARE THE PEOPLE!

WE ARE THE PEOPLE!

WE ARE THE PEOPLE!

WE ARE THE PEOPLE!

E THE OPLE!

WE ARE THE PEOPLE!

WE ARE THE PEOPLE!

THE PROTESTERS CONFRONTED THE STASI COMMANDER IN DRESDEN. THEY FORCED HIM TO OPEN DOORS TO ALL OF THE STASI'S BUILDINGS AND THE LOCAL PRISON.

ACROSS THE STREET, A MERE ONE HUNDRED METERS AWAY, PUTIN WAS WORKING IN THE KGB'S OFFICE.

TWO DOZEN PROTESTERS LEFT THE STASI HEADQUARTERS AND GATHERED OUTSIDE THE KGB VILLA.

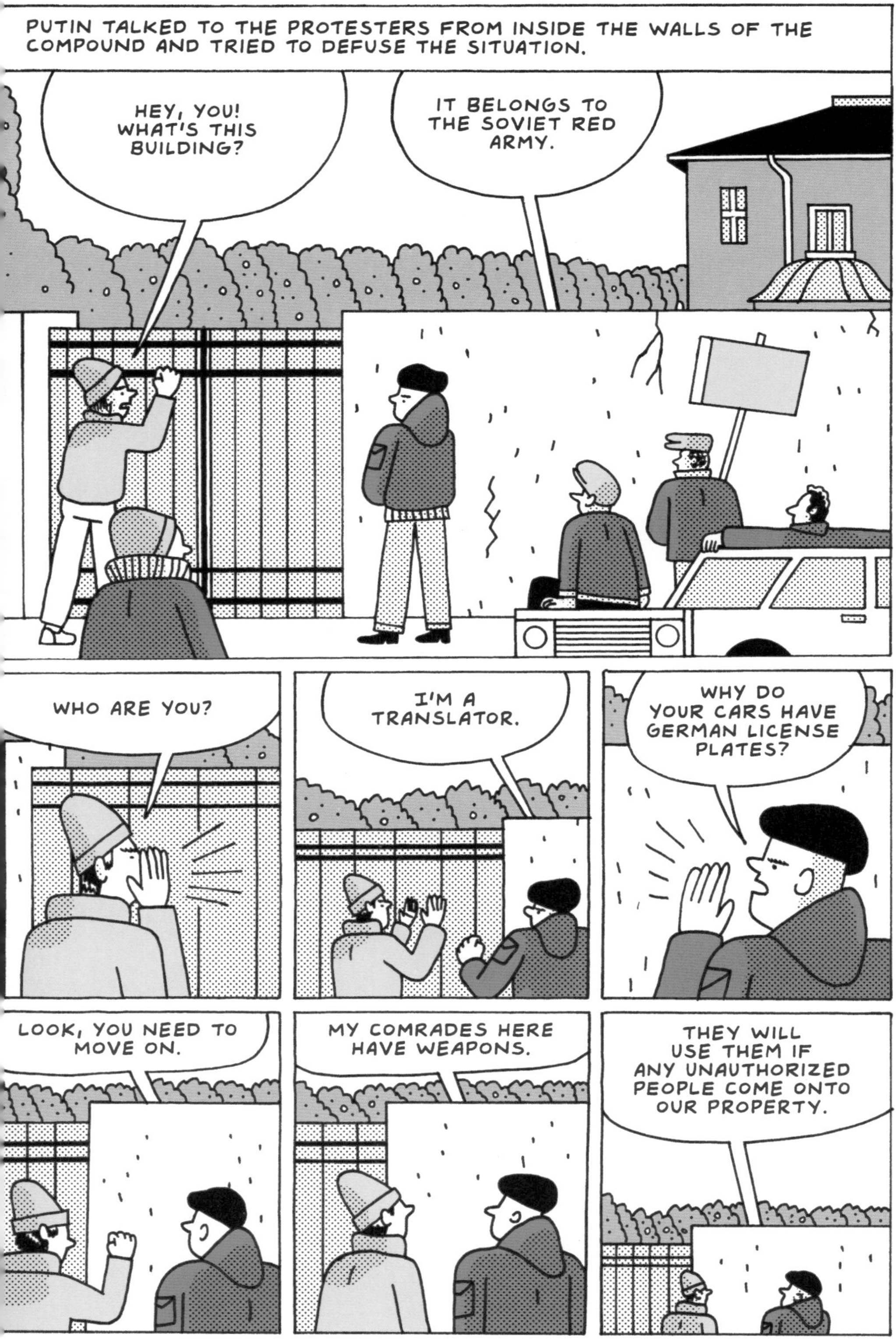
PUTIN TALKED TO THE PROTESTERS FROM INSIDE THE WALLS OF THE COMPOUND AND TRIED TO DEFUSE THE SITUATION.
HEY, YOU! WHAT'S THIS BUILDING?
IT BELONGS TO THE SOVIET RED ARMY.
WHO ARE YOU?
I'M A TRANSLATOR.
WHY DO YOUR CARS HAVE GERMAN LICENSE PLATES?
LOOK, YOU NEED TO MOVE ON.
MY COMRADES HERE HAVE WEAPONS.
THEY WILL USE THEM IF ANY UNAUTHORIZED PEOPLE COME ONTO OUR PROPERTY.

THIS INCIDENT SHOULD HAVE BEEN LOST TO HISTORY. INSTEAD, PUTIN AND KREMLIN PROPAGANDISTS HAVE USED IT TO BOLSTER THE MYTH OF THE RUSSIAN LEADER AS A DARING KGB AGENT ON THE FRONT LINES OF THE COLD WAR.

IN THE KREMLIN'S RETELLING, A HUGE CROWD BROKE THROUGH THE GATES AND STORMED THE GROUNDS.

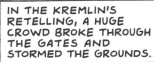

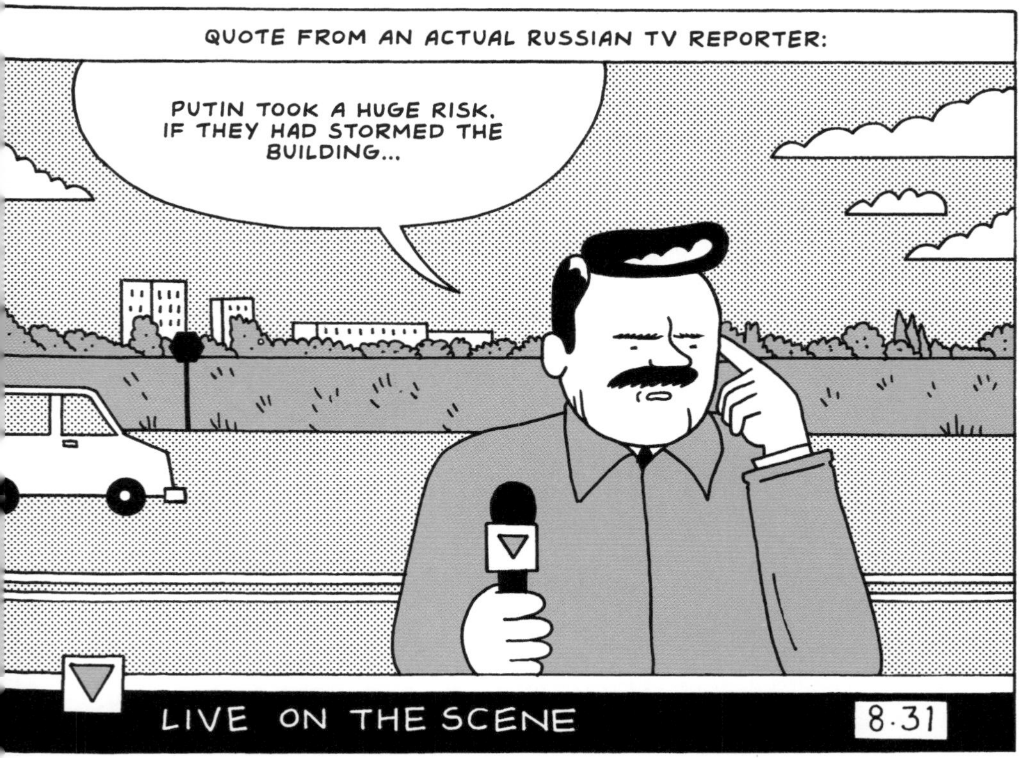
QUOTE FROM AN ACTUAL RUSSIAN TV REPORTER:
PUTIN TOOK A HUGE RISK. IF THEY HAD STORMED THE BUILDING...
LIVE ON THE SCENE
8.31

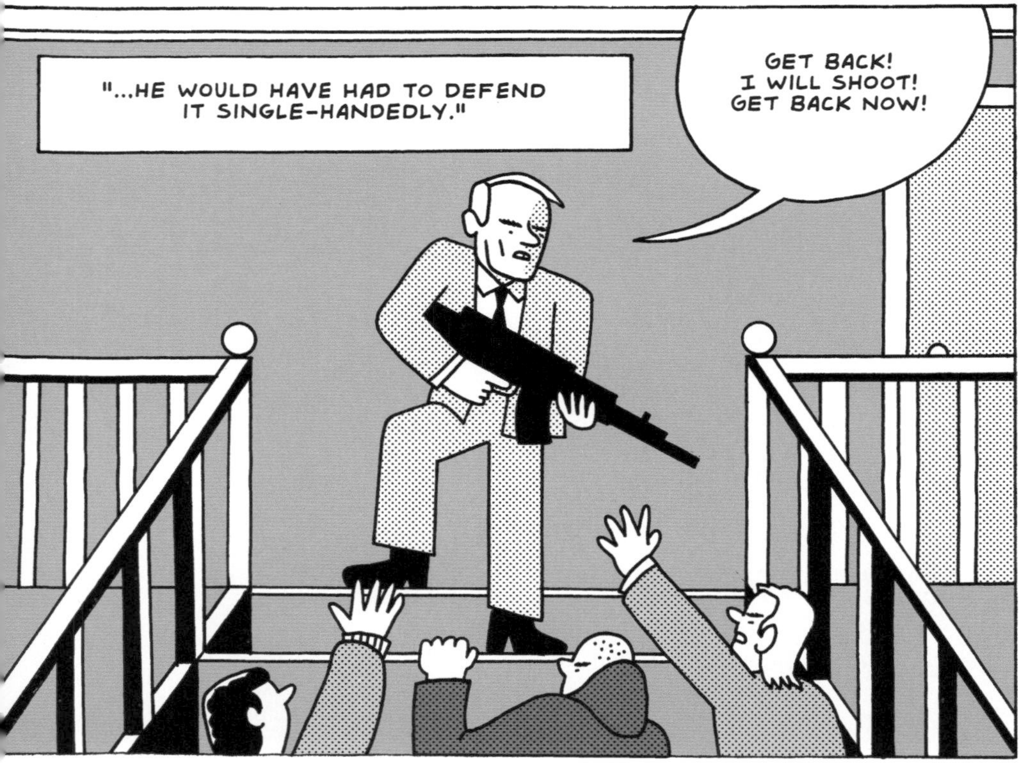
"...HE WOULD HAVE HAD TO DEFEND IT SINGLE-HANDEDLY."
GET BACK! I WILL SHOOT! GET BACK NOW!

IN REALITY, IT WAS A SMALL CROWD. THEY NEVER ENTERED THE COMPOUND. PUTIN CONTACTED THE NEARBY SOVIET MILITARY BASE TO ASK FOR HELP.

THE DUTY OFFICER REBUFFED HIM. THEY COULDN'T STEP IN WITHOUT ORDERS.

MOSCOW IS SILENT.

THE DISARRAY AND PASSIVITY IN THE FACE OF A DANGEROUS, FAST-MOVING SITUATION LEFT A LASTING IMPRESSION.

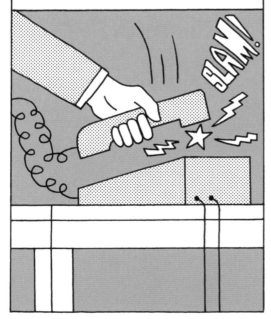

PUTIN SEETHED.

EVENTUALLY, HELP ARRIVED, AND THE PROTESTERS DISPERSED.

FOR THE NEXT SEVERAL DAYS, PUTIN AND HIS FELLOW KGB AGENTS BURNED THEIR FILES.

I PERSONALLY BURNED A HUGE AMOUNT OF MATERIAL.

"WE BURNED SO MUCH STUFF THAT THE FURNACE BURST."

BA-BOOM

THE UNTHINKABLE WAS HAPPENING: THE SOVIET UNION HAD TOTALLY LOST ITS GRIP OVER CENTRAL EUROPE, AND THE TWO GERMANYS WERE UNIFYING.

THE SMALL TEAM OF KGB OFFICERS STATIONED IN DRESDEN NEEDED TO CLOSE UP SHOP AND EVACUATE.

ON THE TRAIN RIDE HOME, PUTIN'S WIFE WAS ROBBED OF HER COAT.

THIEF!

PUTIN'S KGB CAREER WAS EFFECTIVELY OVER.

HE GOT A JOB OFFER AT THE KGB'S MOSCOW HEADQUARTERS. BUT THERE WAS A CATCH: THE KGB DIDN'T PROMISE HIM AN APARTMENT.

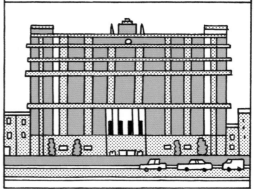

SO HE HEADED BACK HOME TO LENINGRAD.

HE TOLD FRIENDS:

I DON'T KNOW WHAT TO DO.

SOVIET TROOPS AND OFFICIALS RETURNING FROM EASTERN EUROPE MADE A LONG-STANDING HOUSING SHORTAGE EVEN WORSE. SOME SOLDIERS WERE REDUCED TO SLEEPING IN TENTS.

LESS THAN TWO YEARS LATER, IN 1991, THE SOVIET UNION, LIKE EAST GERMANY, ALSO BECAME HISTORY.

THE COUNTRY'S POLITICAL SYSTEM AND ECONOMY WERE MELTING DOWN. BASIC GOODS WERE RATIONED. SHELVES IN STORES WERE TOTALLY EMPTY.

IN FALL 1990, PUTIN FOUND WORK AS THE KGB'S EYES AND EARS AT THE DEAN'S OFFICE OF HIS ALMA MATER...

...LENINGRAD STATE UNIVERSITY.

PUTIN THREW IN WITH THE NEW GENERATION OF REFORMERS RUNNING THE CITY. THEY RESTORED THE CITY'S CZARIST-ERA NAME: ST. PETERSBURG.

ANATOLY SOBCHAK

SOBCHAK, PUTIN'S NEW BOSS, BECAME ST. PETERSBURG'S FIRST ELECTED MAYOR.

THE GOOD-LOOKING SOBCHAK MODELED HIMSELF ON JOHN F. KENNEDY AND DREAMED OF TRANSFORMING ST. PETERSBURG INTO A SHOWCASE OF DEMOCRACY...

...CULTURE...

...AND WESTERN-STYLE CAPITALISM.

LIKE YELTSIN, HE FAILED MISERABLY.

ST. PETERSBURG'S CRIMINALITY AND MAYHEM BECAME A POTENT SYMBOL OF EVERYTHING ROTTEN ABOUT POST-COMMUNIST RUSSIA.

TO BE SURE, CRIMINAL GROUPS HAD OPERATED THROUGHOUT THE SOVIET PERIOD. THEY HELPED RUN THE BLACK MARKET...

...AN ESSENTIAL MECHANISM FOR PROVIDING GOODS THAT THE SCLEROTIC, CENTRALIZED ARMS OF THE STATE COULDN'T HANDLE.

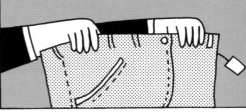

BLAT, THE INFORMAL SOVIET SYSTEM OF DOING FAVORS, AS WELL AS WHEELING AND DEALING FOR HARD-TO-LOCATE GOODS (FOOD, LEVI'S, ETC.), WAS WIDESPREAD.

THE COMMUNIST PARTY AND KGB KEPT CLOSE TABS ON ALL OF THIS...

...OFTEN ESTABLISHING A USEFUL (AND LUCRATIVE) MODUS VIVENDI WITH KEY PLAYERS.

THE COLLAPSE OF THE SOVIET SYSTEM CREATED AN OPENING FOR CORRUPT OFFICIALS, KGB OFFICERS, AND THUGS TO TAKE OVER KEY PARTS OF THE ECONOMY.

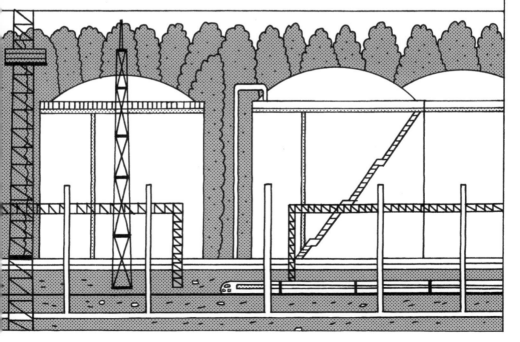

IT WAS THOSE INFORMAL GROUPS, NOT LIBERAL, WELL-INTENTIONED REFORMERS, WHO DOMINATED THE MEAN STREETS AND CASINOS OF "GANGLAND ST. PETERSBURG."

SOON, ST. PETERSBURG, A CITY OF IMPOSING PALACES, CANALS, AND CHURCHES...

...CARVED OUT OF A SWAMP BY CZAR PETER THE GREAT (WITH HELP FROM HUNDREDS OF THOUSANDS OF SLAVE LABORERS)...

...AND THE SITE OF FYODOR DOSTOYEVSKY'S CLASSIC NOVELS...

...WAS AWASH IN BODIES.

THE CITY WAS RUSSIA'S CRIME CAPITAL. THE POLICE LOOKED ON FROM THE SIDELINES.

TOP CITY OFFICIALS, BUSINESSMEN, AND BANKERS WERE GUNNED DOWN IN BROAD DAYLIGHT.

FORMER INTELLIGENCE OFFICERS RENTED THEMSELVES OUT AS HIT MEN.

CRIME LORDS MOVED OUT OF THE SHADOWS, SETTING UP BUSINESSES THAT OFFERED "PROTECTION" FROM RIVAL GANGS.

THESE SERVICES...

...THAT WE PROVIDE...

...COME AT A PRICE.

RUSSIAN OFFICIALS AND ORGANIZED CRIME FIGURES DID LOTS OF SPECIAL FAVORS DURING THE MASSIVE CARVE-UP OF STATE PROPERTY KNOWN AS PRIVATIZATION.

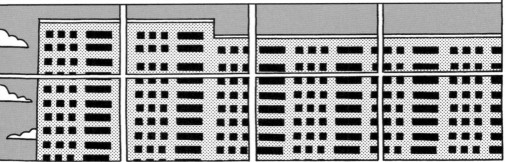

THE MAIN JOB OF THE STATE—PROTECTING RUSSIAN CITIZENS' SAFETY AND WELL-BEING—WAS HANDED OVER TO THE RUSSIAN UNDERWORLD AND ITS PARTNERS.

SOBCHAK AND PUTIN HAD LIMITED POWER. FIGURES LIKE ST. PETERSBURG'S "NIGHTIME GOVERNOR," VLADIMIR KUMARIN, THE ALL-POWERFUL BOSS OF THE NOTORIOUS TAMBOV GANG, WERE THE REAL LAW OF THE LAND.

THEY LAID CLAIM TO VALUABLE ASSETS LIKE ST. PETERSBURG'S FUEL MARKET...

...AND THE CITY'S MAIN PORT.

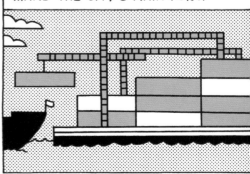

LUXURY CARS, FRESHLY STOLEN OFF THE STREETS OF MAJOR EUROPEAN CITIES, POURED IN.

THE COPS SEIZED MORE THAN A TON OF COCAINE FROM COLOMBIA IN ONE DRUG BUST NEAR ST. PETERSBURG. IT WAS HIDDEN IN 26,000 CANS LABELED "MEAT AND POTATOES."

VIKTOR CHERKESOV, AN OLD FRIEND OF PUTIN'S FROM THEIR KGB DAYS, ANNOUNCED, BIZARRELY, THAT THE COKE WOULD BE HANDED OVER TO THE RUSSIAN STATE STOCKPILE AND BE USED FOR MEDICINAL PURPOSES.

WE WERE DOWN TO JUST ONE KILO STASHED AWAY.*

*HE REALLY SAID THAT.

149

AS THE CITY RAN SHORT ON FOOD AND BASIC GOODS LIKE CIGARETTES, THE SITUATION GOT INCREASINGLY DESPERATE.

POLITICIANS AND BUREAUCRATS IN ST. PETERSBURG WERE EASILY TEMPTED BY PROFITEERING AND CORRUPT SCHEMES.

PUTIN'S STAR ROSE.

HE EVENTUALLY BECAME DEPUTY MAYOR AND WAS PUT IN CHARGE OF DEALINGS WITH FOREIGN COMPANIES.

SOMETIMES HE SLEPT WITH A SHOTGUN.

AT THE TIME, THE FASTEST PATH TO RICHES WAS TO BUY SOMETHING VALUABLE (AT HEAVILY SUBSIDIZED SOVIET PRICES) LIKE OIL OR GASOLINE...

...AND THEN SELL IT OVERSEAS FOR HARD CURRENCY.

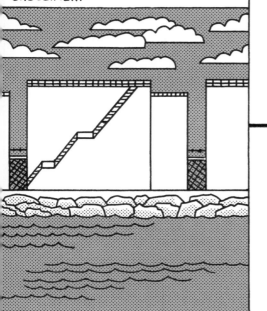

ST. PETERSBURG GOT PERMISSION TO SELL RAW MATERIALS ABROAD ON ITS OWN TO BUY FOOD IN BARTER DEALS. THE MAN IN CHARGE?

HE STEERED SOME OF THOSE CUSHY DEALS TO PALS LIKE GENNADY TIMCHENKO, AN OIL TRADER WHO IS NOW RUSSIA'S FIFTH RICHEST MAN.

PUTIN.

THE MAYOR'S TEAM FORMALLY NOTIFIED MOSCOW ABOUT SALES OF COMMODITIES LIKE FUEL, TIMBER, AND METALS, BUT EVERYTHING WAS RUN OUT OF ST. PETERSBURG.

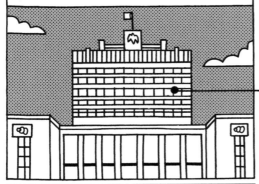
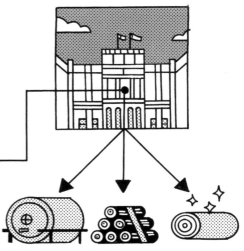

WITHIN THIS DECENTRALIZED SYSTEM, THERE WAS OPPORTUNITY FOR MAKING BIG MONEY. FOR EXAMPLE, ONE DAY, SOBCHAK ASKED TIMCHENKO FOR HELP.

GUYS, WE HAVE FOOD FOR ONLY TWO DAYS, PLEASE DO SOMETHING QUICKLY.

TIMCHENKO ARRANGED TO SELL HEAVY FUEL OIL TO ICELAND...

...IN EXCHANGE FOR SEVERAL TONS OF HERRING.

HOWEVER, RUSSIAN INVESTIGATORS IN THE EARLY 1990S DETERMINED THAT THE PROFITS FROM SOME OF THESE DEALS WERE SIPHONED OFF AND THAT THE PROMISED FOOD SUPPLIES WERE NEVER DELIVERED.

NOWADAYS PUTIN AND TIMCHENKO AMUSE THEMSELVES BY PLAYING EXHIBITION HOCKEY MATCHES WITH LEGENDARY SOVIET AND NHL PLAYERS.

EVENTUALLY, ANTI-CORRUPTION INVESTIGATORS FROM THE CITY COUNCIL AND MOSCOW TRIED TO FIGURE OUT WHAT HAD HAPPENED TO THE MISSING MONEY.

BUT SOBCHAK STONEWALLED REQUESTS TO REFER PUTIN'S CASE TO PROSECUTORS.

BEFORE TOO LONG, THOUGH, SOBCHAK HIMSELF WAS VOTED OUT OF OFFICE.

SOBCHA**T**
FOR MAYOR

PUTIN, AT AGE FORTY-THREE, WAS BACK OUT ON THE STREET WITH ZERO CAREER PROSPECTS.

JUNE 1996

HE TOLD A FRIEND WHO OWNED A JUDO STUDIO:

I MIGHT WANT A JOB AS A TRAINER...IF I DON'T END UP DRIVING A CAB.

AS HE PONDERED HIS NEXT MOVE, A FIRE THAT DESTROYED HIS VACATION HOUSE ADDED INSULT TO INJURY.

PUTIN DASHED INTO THE FLAMES TO RESCUE ONE OF HIS DAUGHTERS AND A VISITOR, WHO WERE TRAPPED ON THE SECOND FLOOR...

...ALONG WITH A BRIEFCASE CONTAINING $5,000.

PUTIN WAS ONCE AGAIN BACKED INTO A CORNER, BUT THIS TIME, THERE WAS NO CLEAR WAY OUT.

CHAPTER
5

FRONTAL ASSAULT

IN DECEMBER 2011, THE STREETS OF MOSCOW ERUPTED WITH PROTESTS AGAINST RIGGED PARLIAMENTARY ELECTIONS.

BUT ELECTION FRAUD UNDER PUTIN WAS NOTHING NEW.

IT WAS PAR FOR THE COURSE IN RUSSIA'S SELF-STYLED "MANAGED DEMOCRACY."

THIS TIME, HOWEVER, ACTIVISTS HAVE CAPTURED BALLOT BOX STUFFING AND OTHER HIJINKS ON THEIR CELL PHONES. THE VIDEOS WENT VIRAL.

ANGER HAD BEEN BUILDING SINCE THE FALL, WHEN PUTIN ANNOUNCED ONE OF HIS TRADEMARK SURPRISES. IN 2008, HE HAD HANDED THE PRESIDENCY OVER TO HIS OLD PAL DMITRI MEDVEDEV.

BUT AT A SPLASHY CONGRESS FOR THE RULING PARTY IN SEPTEMBER 2011, MEDVEDEV AND PUTIN TOOK THE STAGE TOGETHER, AND PUTIN ANNOUNCED THAT HE WAS GOING TO RETURN TO THE PRESIDENCY.

AT THE PARTY CONGRESS, PUTIN OPENLY BRAGGED THAT MEDVEDEV'S BENCHWARMER STINT IN THE JOB WAS MERELY AN ELABORATE HOAX TO CIRCUMVENT TERM LIMITS IN THE RUSSIAN CONSTITUTION.

I WANT TO SAY DIRECTLY—AN AGREEMENT OVER WHAT TO DO IN THE FUTURE WAS REACHED BETWEEN US SEVERAL YEARS AGO.

AND SO, EVEN WITH ALL THE VOTE-STUFFING, THE RULING PARTY STILL UNDERPERFORMED. PUTIN'S RETURN TO THE KREMLIN AND THE ELECTION SHENANIGANS WERE A MAJOR AFFRONT TO THE DIGNITY OF THE REGIME'S BIGGEST BENEFICIARIES...

UNITED RUSSIA PARTY TRIUMPHS   00:52

...THE WELL-TO-DO AND MIDDLE-CLASS RESIDENTS OF MAJOR CITIES LIKE MOSCOW AND ST. PETERSBURG.

AS STREET DEMONSTRATIONS SPREAD ACROSS RUSSIA, PUTIN PANICKED.

ALL YEAR LONG HE'D BEEN WATCHING AS THE MIDDLE EAST WAS ENGULFED BY PROTESTS AND VIOLENCE DURING THE ARAB SPRING.

WAS RUSSIA NEXT?

PUTIN WAS WORRIED THAT MEDVEDEV AND OTHER LIBERAL VOICES INSIDE THE GOVERNMENT WERE TIRED OF HIM AND WANTED TO PUSH HIM OUT.

DON'T ROCK THE BOAT
IT IS
MAKING OUR
RATS NAUSEOUS

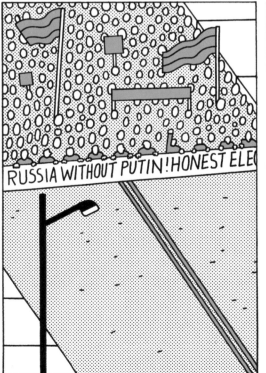

RUSSIA WITHOUT PUTIN! HONEST ELE[

PUTIN AND HIS TEAM QUICKLY
COUNTERATTACKED USING
TRIED-AND-TRUE TACTICS.

PUTIN CLAIMED THAT IT WAS ALL AMERICA'S FAULT. IN REALITY, THE PROTESTS WERE A SPONTANEOUS REACTION FROM PEOPLE WHO FELT THEIR RIGHTS WERE BEING TRAMPLED UPON.

U.S. SECRETARY OF STATE HILLARY CLINTON...

...SET THE TONE FOR SOME ACTORS IN OUR COUNTRY AND GAVE THEM A SIGNAL.

THEY HEARD THE SIGNAL, AND WITH THE SUPPORT OF THE U.S. STATE DEPARTMENT, BEGAN ACTIVE WORK.

IN THE KREMLIN'S RETELLING, THE STREET PROTESTS WERE PART OF A SECRET PLOT BY EVILDOERS IN WASHINGTON.

THEY LAUNCHED VICIOUS ATTACKS ON NEWLY ARRIVED U.S. AMBASSADOR MIKE MCFAUL, A STANFORD PROFESSOR AND AUTHORITY ON DEMOCRATIZATION.

RUSSIAN TV SAID HE'D BEEN SENT TO BE THE RINGLEADER OF THE OPPOSITION MOVEMENT.

THE DISINFORMATION CAMPAIGN WAS RELENTLESS—AND GROTESQUE. A VIRAL VIDEO ACCUSED MCFAUL OF BEING A PEDOPHILE.

AS WE'VE EXPLORED, PUTIN'S FEAR OF COLOR REVOLUTIONS IS NO ACT.

BUT IN THIS CASE, THE OUTPOURING OF ANTI-AMERICANISM WAS ALSO A PLOY TO MOBILIZE SUPPORT FOR PUTIN'S 2012 REELECTION CAMPAIGN...

Ваш голос нужен для победы!

AND TO MARGINALIZE HIS OPPONENTS.

RESIGN PUTIN

THE KREMLIN CRACKED DOWN HARD ON THE PROTESTERS...

...CIVIL SOCIETY ORGANIZATIONS...

...AND THE REMNANTS OF RUSSIA'S INDEPENDENT MEDIA.

NGOS RECEIVING FUNDS FROM ABROAD WERE LABELED "FOREIGN AGENTS."

IN RUSSIA, THE TERM IS SYNONYMOUS WITH "SPIES AND TRAITORS."

PROTESTERS WERE PORTRAYED ON STATE MEDIA AS OUT OF TOUCH, SPOILED BRATS...

...AND LIMOUSINE LIBERALS.

TATNEFT

THE HARASSMENT CAMPAIGN THAT HAPPENED ONLINE WAS JUST AS INTENSE.

OPPOSITION POLITICIANS, ACTIVISTS, AND JOURNALISTS WERE BARRAGED BY LEAKS OF EMBARRASSING INFORMATION, TROLLS, AND FAKE NEWS.

IN EARLY 2012, RUSSIAN JOURNALISTS MOCKED RUSSIAN POLITICAL OPPOSITION FIGURES OUTSIDE THE U.S. EMBASSY AS THEY ARRIVED FOR A MEETING WITH MCFAUL.

TV CREWS ALSO REGULARLY "DOORSTEPPED" MCFAUL WHILE HE WAS ON THE WAY TO PRIVATE MEETINGS. AT ONE POINT, HE UTTERED...

RUSSIA IS A WILD COUNTRY.

HE LATER APOLOGIZED.

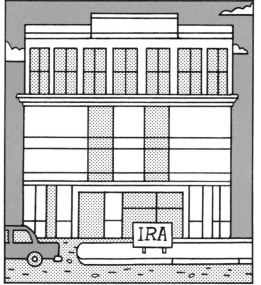

IT WOULD BE SEVERAL YEARS BEFORE AMERICANS LEARNED ABOUT QUASI-PRIVATE OUTFITS, LIKE THE INTERNET RESEARCH AGENCY, THAT DID THE KREMLIN'S DIRTY WORK.

IRA

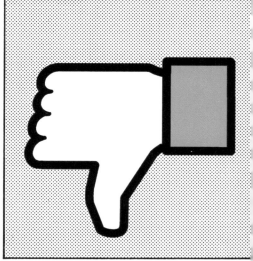

DURING THE UPROAR ABOUT RUSSIAN INTERFERENCE IN THE 2016 PRESIDENTIAL ELECTION, HARDLY ANYONE IN THE WEST REGISTERED THE FACT THAT THESE TOOLS WERE ALL ORIGINALLY CREATED TO NEUTRALIZE PUTIN'S DOMESTIC OPPONENTS.

PUTIN'S IMAGE GOT AN EXTREME MAKEOVER.

MANY EURO-ATLANTIC COUNTRIES HAVE MOVED AWAY FROM THEIR ROOTS, INCLUDING CHRISTIAN VALUES.

HIS MORALIZING HAD A POLITICAL PURPOSE: TO DRAW A STRONG CONTRAST WITH THE PRO-WESTERN LEADERS OF THE PROTEST MOVEMENT.

POLICIES ARE BEING PURSUED THAT PLACE ON THE SAME LEVEL A MULTI-CHILD FAMILY AND A SAME-SEX PARTNERSHIP...

...A FAITH IN GOD AND A BELIEF IN SATAN. THIS IS THE PATH TO DEGRADATION.

A LAW BANNING "GAY PROPAGANDA" (WHATEVER THAT IS) SAILED THROUGH THE DUMA.

THE STRANGE CASE OF PUSSY RIOT BECAME A POTENT SYMBOL OF THE CRACKDOWN ON FREE SPEECH AND OPPOSITION FIGURES.

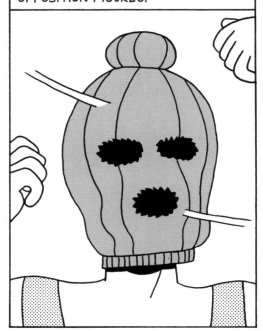

IN THE SUMMER OF 2011, A GROUP OF ARTISTS AND STUDENTS CREATED A FEMINIST PUNK BAND.

THEY VIDEOTAPED PERFORMANCES AROUND MOSCOW LACED WITH ANTI-PUTIN MESSAGING.

A STUNT AT THE CITY'S LARGEST ORTHODOX CATHEDRAL BACKFIRED SPECTACULARLY.

VIRGIN MARY MOTHER OF GOD

BANISH PUTIN, BANISH PUTIN, BANISH PUTIN

THE MEMBERS OF THE GROUP WERE ARRESTED FOR HOOLIGANISM AND INCITING RELIGIOUS HATRED.

THEY WERE MAKING A VIDEO OF A PERFORMANCE CALLED "PUNK PRAYER"...

SHIT!

SHIT!!

HOLY SHIT!!

...INSIDE THE CATHEDRAL OF CHRIST THE SAVIOR.

THE ENTIRE SPECTACLE ENDED UP SERVING THE KREMLIN'S PURPOSES AND ADVANCED A SIMPLE MESSAGE: PUTIN'S OPPONENTS—EVERY SINGLE ONE OF THEM—ARE JUST LIKE PUSSY RIOT. THEY ARE, CERTIFIABLY:

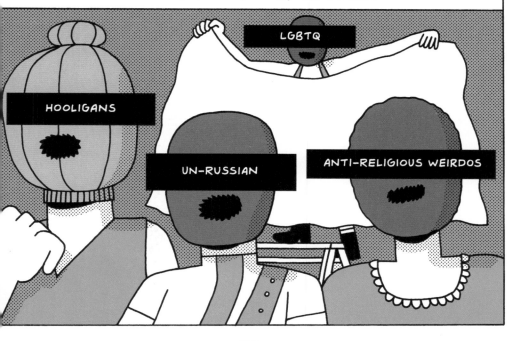

LGBTQ

HOOLIGANS

UN-RUSSIAN

ANTI-RELIGIOUS WEIRDOS

THE PUSSY RIOT TRIAL MADE WAVES IN THE WEST.

BUT THAT DIDN'T BOTHER ANYONE IN THE KREMLIN.

MADONNA

THEIR GOAL WAS TO CONVINCE AVERAGE RUSSIANS THAT WANTING DEMOCRACY OR AN ALTERNATIVE TO PUTIN WAS...

...HE'S GIVEN HIS FRIENDS HALF THE COUNTRY!

CAMEO ON *HOUSE OF CARDS*

...UN-RUSSIAN—NE NASH! [Не наш!].

THROUGH THEIR ACTIONS AGAINST DISSIDENTS, THE KREMLIN WAS PLAYING ON A CARDINAL PRINCIPLE OF RUSSIAN/SOVIET POLITICAL CULTURE. IT'S A TRIBAL IDEA: "NASH"/"НАШ" (ONE OF OURS) VS. "NE NASH"/"НЕ НАШ" (NOT ONE OF OURS).

AVERAGE RUSSIANS ARE MORE COMFORTABLE DEFINING THEMSELVES THROUGH "NEGATIVE IDENTITY."

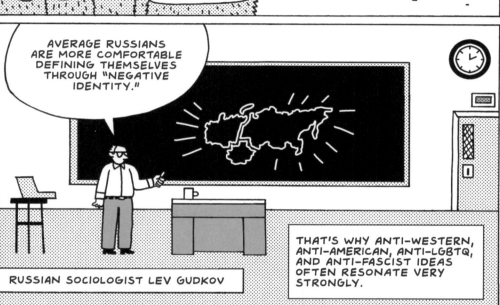

RUSSIAN SOCIOLOGIST LEV GUDKOV

THAT'S WHY ANTI-WESTERN, ANTI-AMERICAN, ANTI-LGBTQ, AND ANTI-FASCIST IDEAS OFTEN RESONATE VERY STRONGLY.

RUSSIA, A MULTIETHNIC EMPIRE THROUGHOUT MOST OF ITS HISTORY, HAS LONG SUFFERED FROM A BIT OF AN IDENTITY CRISIS.

UNLIKE AMERICANS' CORE VALUES LIKE "LIFE, LIBERTY, AND THE PURSUIT OF HAPPINESS"...

...THE VERY IDEA OF WHAT MAKES RUSSIA *RUSSIA* HAS NEVER BEEN FIXED IN STONE.

AS THE RUSSIAN STATE MATURED, LEADERS AND THINKERS STARTED TO EMBRACE A MESSIANIC IDEA OF RUSSIAN EXCEPTIONALISM—MOSCOW AS THE THIRD ROME.

RUSSIA WILL BE AN EMPIRE, A CIVILIZATION.

THAT IDEA IGNITED THE IMAGINATIONS OF CZARS, KOMISSARS, MEMBERS OF THE ELITE, AND WRITERS LIKE DOSTOYEVSKY FOR RUSSIA TO PLAY A UNIQUE ROLE ON THE WORLD STAGE AND TO FOLLOW A "SPECIAL PATH."

IT ALSO PUT TERRITORIAL EXPANSION AT THE CORE OF RUSSIA'S NATIONAL IDENTITY.

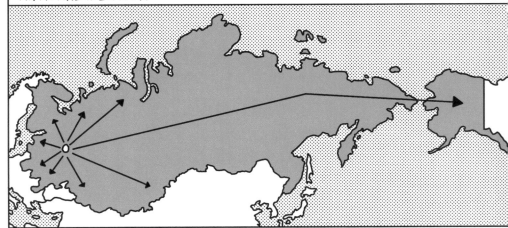

FEBRUARY 2012, PUTIN CAMPAIGN APPEARANCE

WE WILL NOT ALLOW SOMEONE TO IMPOSE THEIR WILL ON US BECAUSE WE HAVE OUR OWN WILL!

PUTIN HAS RALLIED RUSSIANS AROUND THE IDEA THAT THEIR "SPECIAL PATH" IS ALL ABOUT ANTI-AMERICANISM AND STANDING UP TO AN OUT-OF-CONTROL U.S. THAT WANTS TO MESS AROUND IN RUSSIA'S INTERNAL AFFAIRS.

WE ARE A VICTORIOUS PEOPLE! IT IS IN OUR GENES AND IN OUR GENETIC CODE!

173

GUDKOV EXPLAINS THAT ANTI-WESTERN SENTIMENT LIKE THAT EXPRESSED BY PUTIN HELPS RUSSIANS GET OVER...

THE TRAUMAS OF RUSSIAN COLLECTIVE CONSCIOUSNESS

COMPLEXES ASSOCIATED WITH LOW NATIONAL SELF-ESTEEM...

"...A SENSE OF THE BACKWARDNESS OF THE COUNTRY..."

"...POVERTY..."

"...THE FAILURE OF ECONOMIC AND SOCIAL REFORMS..."

"...THE END OF THE DEMOCRATIC TRANSITION [OF THE 1990S], ETC."

PUTIN'S TACTICS AND FLAMBOYANT EMBRACE OF RUSSIAN NATIONALISM HAVE STRONG HISTORICAL ANTECEDENTS.

IN DECEMBER 1825, A LOOSELY ORGANIZED GROUP OF RUSSIAN LIBERAL MILITARY OFFICERS AND ARISTOCRATS WHO CALLED THEMSELVES THE DECEMBRISTS TRIED TO OVERTHROW CZAR NICHOLAS I.

GASP!

INFLUENCED BY THE IDEAS OF 17TH- AND 18TH-CENTURY EUROPEAN INTELLECTUALS, MOST OF THE DECEMBRISTS PARTICIPATED IN SECRET SOCIETIES. THEY MADE VARIOUS DEMANDS:

A CONSTITUTIONAL MONARCHY!

THE RULE OF LAW!

EQUAL RIGHTS!

A FREELY ELECTED PARLIAMENT!

AN END TO SERFDOM!

NICHOLAS I'S REGIME RUTHLESSLY CRUSHED THE BADLY ORGANIZED MUTINY. A SMALL HANDFUL OF THE DECEMBRISTS WERE EXECUTED.

MOST OF THEM WERE SENT INTO EXILE IN INHOSPITABLE PLACES LIKE SIBERIA. DECEMBRISTS WHO CAME FROM THE ARISTOCRACY WERE STRIPPED OF THEIR PROPERTY AND NOBLE TITLES.

THE HEROISM AND SACRIFICE OF THE DECEMBRISTS AND THEIR FAMILIES WERE LATER TAUGHT TO GENERATIONS OF RUSSIAN SCHOOLCHILDREN.

HEROES.

LENIN CELEBRATED THEM AS THE PRECURSORS OF THE BOLSHEVIKS WHO LED THE 1917 OCTOBER REVOLUTION.

BUT AT THE TIME, NICHOLAS I, A STAUNCH SUPPORTER OF AUTOCRACY, TOOK RUSSIA IN A REACTIONARY DIRECTION AFTER THE DECEMBRISTS' REVOLT.

HE OPPOSED LIMITS ON HIS POWERS OR THE GRANTING OF ANY RIGHTS TO SOCIETY AS A WHOLE.

INSTEAD, HE TIGHTENED THE SCREWS...

...AND ESTABLISHED THE FORERUNNER OF RUSSIA'S SECRET POLICE, THE THIRD DEPARTMENT.

HE REIGNED FOR THIRTY YEARS.

BANG

RUSSIA DODGED THE 1848 WAVE OF NATIONALIST UPRISINGS THAT HIT FRANCE, GERMANY, ITALY, THE AUSTRO-HUNGARIAN EMPIRE, AND OTHER PARTS OF EUROPE.

HOWEVER, THROUGHOUT NICHOLAS I'S REIGN, MISTRUST BETWEEN THE CZARIST REGIME AND THE RUSSIAN ELITE WORSENED.

AUTHORS, FREE THINKERS, AND POETS RETREATED INTO THE WORLD OF LITERATURE AND IDEAS.

THEY WROTE ESSAYS, CREATED DEBATE SOCIETIES, AND JOINED SALONS.

THE GOLDEN AGE OF RUSSIAN LITERATURE BUILT MOMENTUM...

...WHILE THE CZAR'S THIRD DEPARTMENT KEPT CLOSE WATCH.

EMINENT WRITERS SUCH AS ALEKSANDR PUSHKIN, NIKOLAI GOGOL, MIKHAIL LERMONTOV, ALEKSANDR HERZEN, AND IVAN TURGENEV ALL FACED POLITICAL TROUBLE AND PRESSURE FROM THE CZAR'S CENSORS.

PUSHKIN HAD TO SUBMIT HIS POEMS TO CZAR NICHOLAS I TO BE REVIEWED BEFORE PUBLICATION.

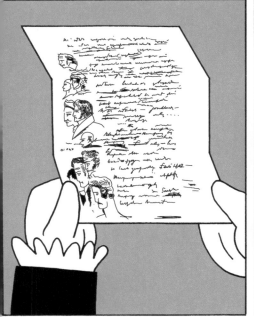

THE CZAR USUALLY FOBBED OFF MOST OF THE ACTUAL WORK TO THE HEAD OF THE SECRET POLICE:

COUNT VON BENCKENDORFF.

PYOTR CHAADAYEV, A PROMINENT ARISTOCRAT, WAS DECLARED CRIMINALLY INSANE BY BENCKENDORFF FOR PUBLISHING AN ATTACK ON RUSSIA'S BACKWARDNESS.

CZAR NICHOLAS I REACTED HARSHLY TO AN ARTICLE ABOUT THE EDUCATION SYSTEM, WRITING TO ONE OF HIS MINISTERS...

DURING NICHOLAS I'S REIGN, RUSSIA GOT AN OFFICIAL IDEOLOGY FOR THE FIRST TIME IN ITS HISTORY. IT WAS ALL OF THREE WORDS: ORTHODOXY, AUTOCRACY, NATIONALITY.

FOR PUTIN, THESE WORDS FIT LIKE A GLOVE, OF COURSE. AS WE DISCUSSED EARLIER, A STRONG CENTRALIZED GOVERNMENT HAS BEEN THE NORM IN RUSSIA FOR CENTURIES.

QUITE UNDERSTANDABLY, PUTIN HAS BEEN SEEN AS THE PERSON WHO KILLED OFF RUSSIA'S FLEDGLING DEMOCRACY. HOWEVER, THIS PERIOD OF FREEWHEELING (AND OFTEN CHAOTIC) PRO-WESTERN REFORMS DURING THE 1990S WAS LARGELY A HISTORICAL ANOMALY.

BY THE TIME PUTIN TOOK OFFICE, A GREAT MANY MEMBERS OF THE ELITE BELIEVED THAT BOTCHED LIBERALIZATION AND DECENTRALIZATION HAD PUSHED THINGS OUT OF CONTROL.

AVERTING RUSSIA'S COLLAPSE BECAME THE NORTH STAR FOR PUTIN AND THE SO-CALLED *DERZHAVNIKI* (SUPPORTERS OF RUSSIA'S GREAT POWER STATUS) WHO SURROUNDED HIM.

THEIR OVERRIDING GOALS HAVE BEEN TO MAINTAIN STABILITY, PROTECT THEIR POWER, AND KEEP RUSSIA'S TRADITIONAL ENEMIES OFF-BALANCE.

IN 2013, AN OPPORTUNITY TO ADVANCE THAT FINAL GOAL FELL INTO THE KREMLIN'S LAP...

...EDWARD SNOWDEN.

SNOWDEN, A FORMER CONTRACTOR FOR THE NATIONAL SECURITY AGENCY (NSA), WAS ON THE RUN FROM THE FBI. THE KREMLIN WARMLY WELCOMED HIM.

Эдвард СНОУден

WESTERN MEDIA WERE THRILLED BY THE CHANCE TO PUBLISH THE ARCHIVE OF TOP-SECRET NSA DOCUMENTS STOLEN BY SNOWDEN.

IT WAS A NICE PREVIEW OF HOW THE KREMLIN WOULD WEAPONIZE THE MEDIA THREE YEARS LATER...

...WHEN WIKILEAKS STARTED RELEASING HACKED EMAILS FROM THE HILLARY CLINTON CAMPAIGN.

 Donald J. Trump
@REALDONALDTRUMP   [8 +FOLLOW]

VERY LITTLE PICK-UP BY THE DISHONEST MEDIA OF INCREDIBLE INFORMATION PROVIDED BY WIKILEAKS. SO DISHONEST! RIGGED SYSTEM!

RETWEETS   LIKES
22,765   54,964

IN INTERVIEWS, SNOWDEN DODGED UNCOMFORTABLE QUESTIONS ABOUT RUSSIA'S RUTHLESS INTELLIGENCE SERVICES AND ABYSMAL HUMAN RIGHTS RECORD.

INSTEAD, WESTERN MEDIA AND PUBLIC OPINION FOCUSED ON THE IMPLICATIONS OF THE NSA'S MASSIVE DOMESTIC AND GLOBAL SURVEILLANCE PROGRAMS.

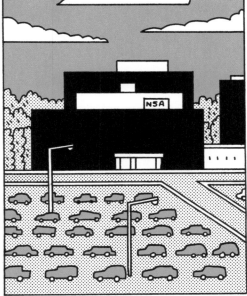

THE SNOWDEN AFFAIR HARMED INTERNATIONAL CONFIDENCE IN THE U.S.

THE DISCOVERY THAT THE NSA HAD WIRETAPPED CHANCELLOR ANGELA MERKEL'S CELL PHONE CREATED A POLITICAL FIRESTORM AROUND THE WORLD AND CAUSED LONG-TERM DAMAGE TO U.S.–GERMAN RELATIONS.

SO WHO WAS THE BAD GUY NOW— OBAMA OR PUTIN? IT WAS ANOTHER TASTE OF THE KREMLIN'S WILLINGNESS TO PLAY DIRTY TO HURT ITS ENEMIES.

ALL THE WHILE, PUTIN WAS OVERSEEING PREPARATIONS FOR A MASSIVE COMING-OUT PARTY FOR RUSSIA: THE 2014 WINTER OLYMPICS IN SOCHI.

SOCHI IS A SUBTROPICAL RESORT AREA ON THE BLACK SEA...

...AND PUTIN'S FAVORITE VACATION PLAYGROUND.

PUTIN WAS ANGERED WHEN THE GAMES WERE OVERSHADOWED BY NEGATIVE PRESS COVERAGE ABOUT CONSTRUCTION DELAYS...

...TERRORIST THREATS...

...AND THE GOVERNMENT'S ANTI-LGBTQ CAMPAIGN. THE SOCHI GAMES WERE SUPPOSED TO BE A SHOWCASE FOR THE NEW RUSSIA.

PUTIN WAS DOUBLY INFURIATED WHEN OBAMA AND OTHER WESTERN LEADERS DECIDED TO STAY AWAY FROM THE OPENING CEREMONIES. THE WHITE HOUSE NAMED AN OFFICIAL DELEGATION WITH PROMINENT LGBTQ FIGURES LIKE TENNIS LEGEND BILLIE JEAN KING.

BUT THE WORST WAS YET TO COME. IT WAS RIGHT NEXT DOOR IN UKRAINE.

JUST AS THE SOCHI OLYMPICS WERE WRAPPING UP, DOWNTOWN KYIV WAS ENGULFED BY CHAOTIC STREET PROTESTS THAT LOOKED LIKE A REPLAY OF THE 2004 ORANGE REVOLUTION.

YANUKOVYCH, WHO HAD MANAGED TO GET HIMSELF ELECTED PRESIDENT OF UKRAINE A FEW YEARS EARLIER, HAD BEEN ENGAGED IN A DANGEROUS GAME.

HE WAS PLAYING RUSSIA AND THE EUROPEAN UNION OFF OF EACH OTHER, THINKING THAT A BIDDING WAR FOR UKRAINE'S LOYALTY WOULD HELP HIM WIN A REELECTION CAMPAIGN.

IN LATE 2013, PUTIN PROMISED YANUKOVYCH MORE THAN $20 BILLION IN LOANS AND ENERGY SUBSIDIES TO DISSUADE HIM FROM SIGNING AN IMPORTANT TRADE DEAL WITH THE EUROPEANS.

PUTIN BELIEVED HE HAD OUTMANEUVERED EUROPEANS WHO WANTED TO PULL UKRAINE TOWARD THE WEST.

INSTEAD, HE SET IN MOTION A POPULAR REVOLUTION. IT ALL BEGAN WHEN A JOURNALIST ORGANIZED A FACEBOOK MEETUP ON KYIV'S MAIN SQUARE, THE MAIDAN.

 Mustafa Nayyem
November 21, 2013 🌐

Come on guys, let's be serious. If you really want to do something, don't just "like" this post. Write that you are ready, and we can try to start something.

Like Comment Share

THE PROTESTS INITIALLY STAYED SMALL. RUSLANA, UKRAINE'S ANSWER TO SHAKIRA, PUMPED OUT HER SCHLOCKY EURODISCO HITS.

STUDENTS SANG, DANCED, AND DEMANDED YANUKOVYCH'S OUSTER.

A FEW NIGHTS LATER YANUKOVYCH TRIED TO CLEAR THE SQUARE. RIOT POLICE VIOLENTLY ATTACKED THE STUDENTS.

THE NEXT DAY, HUNDREDS OF THOUSANDS OF ANGRY UKRAINIANS CROWDED INTO THE SQUARE.

HAPPY TRAILS!!

A MIDDLE-AGED DOCTOR BERATED POLICE IN THE STREETS.

YOU ARE NOTHING BUT PROSTITUTES!!

THE KREMLIN KEPT PUSHING YANUKOVYCH TO TAKE MORE AGGRESSIVE ACTION, BUT EVERYONE KNEW HE WAS A COWARD. PUTIN HAD UNDOUBTEDLY SEEN AN INFAMOUS VIDEO OF YANUKOVYCH CRUMPLING TO THE GROUND IN 2006...

...AFTER GETTING HIT WITH AN EGG ON THE CAMPAIGN TRAIL AND THINKING IT WAS AN ASSASSIN'S BULLET.

THE STANDOFF ON THE MAIDAN DRAGGED ON FOR MANY WEEKS IN THE DEAD OF WINTER. EVENTUALLY, THE UKRAINIAN GOVERNMENT USED DEADLY FORCE AGAINST ITS OWN PEOPLE.

TROOPS TURNED DOWNTOWN KYIV INTO A WAR ZONE.

SNIPERS OPENED FIRE ON THE DEMONSTRATORS.

ALL HELL BROKE LOOSE.

AT LEAST FIFTY PEOPLE WERE KILLED.

A LAST-DITCH DIPLOMATIC SOLUTION WAS BROKERED BY EUROPEAN DIPLOMATS. IT UNRAVELED IMMEDIATELY.

YANUKOVYCH, A TRUE COWARD TO THE END, FLED THE COUNTRY IN THE MIDDLE OF THE NIGHT.

HE RESURFACED A FEW DAYS LATER IN RUSSIA.

LIVE | RT | OUSTED UKRAINE PRESIDENT | 11:33

PUTIN WAS TAKEN TOTALLY OFF GUARD BY EVENTS IN UKRAINE. FOR DECADES, ARROGANT RUSSIAN OFFICIALS HAD TREATED THE COUNTRY LIKE IT WAS PART OF RUSSIA.

THIS HUBRIS, IN PART, CAUSED PUTIN TO MISREAD THE SITUATION. HE DIDN'T REALIZE HOW DRAMATICALLY THE WINDS HAD SHIFTED.

HE CONVINCED HIMSELF THE REBELLION WAS ANOTHER CIA-SPONSORED COLOR REVOLUTION.

"YOU BELIEVE THE UNITED STATES HAD SOMETHING TO DO WITH THE OUSTING OF YANUKOVYCH, WHEN HE HAD TO FLEE TO RUSSIA?"

Charlie ros

lie rose   charlie rose   charlie rose   charlie r

"I KNOW THIS FOR SURE."

HOW CAN YOU KNOW FOR SURE?

IT IS VERY SIMPLE. WE KNOW WHO HAD MEETINGS AND WORKED WITH PEOPLE WHO OVERTHREW VIKTOR YANUKOVYCH...

...AS WELL AS WHEN AND WHERE THEY DID IT. WE KNOW THE WAYS THE ASSISTANCE WAS PROVIDED, WE KNOW HOW MUCH THEY PAID THEM.

WE KNOW WHICH TERRITORIES AND COUNTRIES HOSTED TRAININGS AND HOW IT WAS DONE. WE KNOW WHO THE INSTRUCTORS WERE. WE KNOW EVERYTHING.

WELL, ACTUALLY, OUR U.S. PARTNERS ARE NOT KEEPING IT A SECRET. THEY OPENLY ADMIT TO PROVIDING ASSISTANCE, TRAINING PEOPLE, AND SPENDING A SPECIFIC AMOUNT OF MONEY ON IT.

THEY ARE NAMING LARGE SUMS OF MONEY: UP TO $5 BILLION—WE ARE TALKING ABOUT BILLIONS OF DOLLARS HERE.

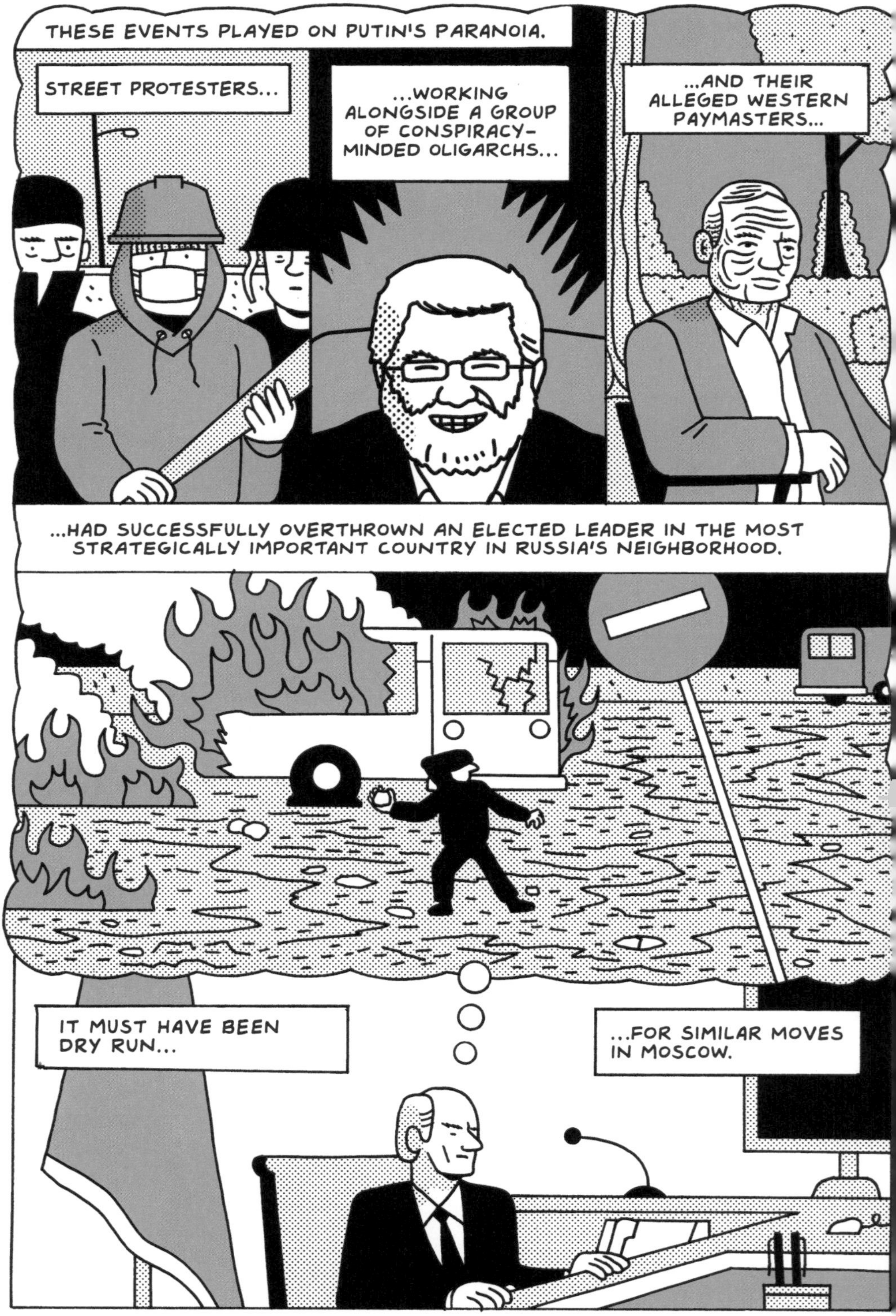
THESE EVENTS PLAYED ON PUTIN'S PARANOIA.
STREET PROTESTERS...
...WORKING ALONGSIDE A GROUP OF CONSPIRACY-MINDED OLIGARCHS...
...AND THEIR ALLEGED WESTERN PAYMASTERS...
...HAD SUCCESSFULLY OVERTHROWN AN ELECTED LEADER IN THE MOST STRATEGICALLY IMPORTANT COUNTRY IN RUSSIA'S NEIGHBORHOOD.
IT MUST HAVE BEEN DRY RUN...
...FOR SIMILAR MOVES IN MOSCOW.

AFTER AN ALL-NIGHT MEETING WITH HIS INNER CIRCLE, PUTIN DECIDED TO REASSERT HIS DOMINANCE IN THE REGION BY SEIZING CRIMEA, A UKRAINIAN TERRITORY.

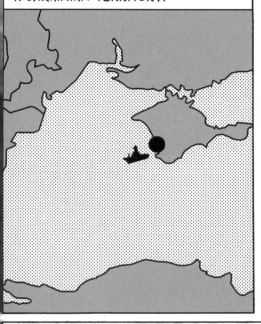

IT WAS (AND STILL IS) HOME TO A MAJOR RUSSIAN NAVAL BASE...

...AND A LARGE POPULATION OF PRO-MOSCOW MILITARY RETIREES.

PUTIN WANTED TO MAKE SURE THAT UKRAINE COULDN'T JUMP DECISIVELY INTO THE WESTERN CAMP. BY PUTTING PRESSURE ON THE NATIONALIST-LED INTERIM GOVERNMENT, HE HOPED THAT THE REVOLUTION WOULD COLLAPSE.

THE CRIMEA OPERATION WAS A SHOWCASE FOR RUSSIA'S NEW MILITARY AND INTELLIGENCE CAPABILITIES.

MASKED SOLDIERS WITHOUT INSIGNIA POPPED UP ALL OVER.

THE KREMLIN DISOWNED ANY RESPONSIBILITY.

JOURNALISTS AND PRO-KREMLIN MOUTHPIECES CALLED THEM "LITTLE GREEN MEN" OR "POLITE PEOPLE..."

...BUT THEY WERE REALLY RUSSIAN SPECIAL FORCES.

PUTIN CLAIMED THAT THE SOLDIERS WEARING THE LATEST TOP-OF-THE-LINE GEAR WERE JUST LOCALS WHO COULD HAVE BOUGHT THEIR UNIFORMS OFF THE SHELF AT ANY STORE.

THE U.S. AND EUROPE WERE CAUGHT FLAT-FOOTED. PUTIN GUESSED—CORRECTLY—THAT THE WEST HAD NO INTEREST IN A DIRECT MILITARY CONFRONTATION.

HE FORMALLY ANNEXED THE TERRITORY. IN THE EYES OF MOST RUSSIANS, A GREAT HISTORICAL INJUSTICE WAS BEING REVERSED.

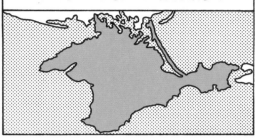

CRIMEA HAD BEEN ARBITRARILY HANDED OVER TO UKRAINE DURING THE 1950S BY NIKITA KHRUSHCHEV AT A TIME WHEN THE SOVIET UNION'S INTERNAL BORDERS WERE LARGELY A FORMALITY.

PUTIN HAD TAPPED INTO THE SENSE OF GRIEVANCE AND VICTIMHOOD ABOUT THE END OF THE COLD WAR THAT HIS GOVERNMENT HAD BEEN INSTILLING IN RUSSIANS SINCE 2000.

THIS TIME AROUND, PUTIN WAS STICKING IT TO THE WEST: RUSSIA WOULD BE HUMILIATED NO MORE.

NEVER MIND THAT PUTIN HAD TOTALLY BOTCHED THINGS IN UKRAINE—FOR A SECOND TIME. SEIZING CRIMEA WAS A POLITICAL MASTERSTROKE.

PUTIN'S APPROVAL RATING SOARED TO STRATOSPHERIC LEVELS AT NEAR 90%.

HIS DOMESTIC OPPONENTS WERE VAPORIZED.

THE RUSSIAN STATE PROPAGANDA APPARATUS WENT INTO OVERDRIVE. THE UKRAINIAN REVOLUTION WAS A CIA-BACKED, NAZI-LED COUP D'ÉTAT.

RUSSIAN TV VIEWERS WERE BOMBARDED WITH OVER-THE-TOP REPORTS ABOUT THE CONFLICT.

IN THE KREMLIN'S NEW LEXICON, THE WORD *MAIDAN* BECAME AN OBSCENITY. UKRAINIANS WERE MORPHED INTO BLOODTHIRSTY FASCISTS.

STATE TV EVEN CLAIMED THAT A THREE-YEAR-OLD BOY WAS PUBLICLY CRUCIFIED ON A CITY SQUARE BY UKRAINIAN SOLDIERS...

...TO PUNISH HIS FAMILY FOR SIDING WITH MOSCOW.

RUSSIAN TV SPOTLIGHTED PUBLIC DISPLAY OF THE CONTROVERSIAL RED-AND-BLACK FLAG OF UKRAINE'S 1940S FASCIST MOVEMENT, THE UKRAINIAN INSURGENT ARMY.

ACCORDING TO RUSSIAN PROPAGANDA, THE UKRAINIAN REVOLUTION WASN'T A SPONTANEOUS EVENT. IT WAS "MADE IN THE USA." A SENIOR STATE DEPARTMENT OFFICIAL WAS SHOWN HANDING OUT COOKIES TO PROTESTERS ON THE MAIDAN.

JOHN MCCAIN, PERENNIAL PUTIN NEMESIS, HAD ADDRESSED A CROWD OF HUNDREDS OF THOUSANDS OF PROTESTERS.

AMERICA IS WITH YOU! I AM WITH YOU!

THE KREMLIN'S RALLYING CRY BECAME "KRYM NASH!"

CRIMEA IS OURS!

★★★★★
PUTIN
MADE RUSSIA GREAT AGAIN!
★★★★★

THE APPEAL OF "KRYM NASH!" WAS INTOXICATING FOR PUTIN'S SUPPORTERS.

CRIMEA— IN MY HEART

MY LIBERAL RUSSIAN FRIENDS STARTED TO CALL THOSE PEOPLE KRYM-NASHI ("CRIMEA'S OURS"-NIKS) MUCH AS AMERICAN LIBERALS CALL DONALD TRUMP'S FANS MAGAS.

RUSSIAN PROPAGANDA WAS NOT SUBTLE.

OR

NOR WAS THE RACIST IMAGERY OF ANTI-OBAMA BILLBOARDS THAT POPPED UP IN MOSCOW.

BANANA   OBAMA
UKRAINE
DON'T CHOKE ON IT

THE SEIZURE OF CRIMEA CREATED AN ENTIRELY NEW REALITY—BOTH FOR RUSSIAN POLITICS AND FOR THE SECURITY OF EUROPE.

POST-COLD-WAR ILLUSIONS WERE SHATTERED OVERNIGHT. POSTCOMMUNIST RUSSIA WAS NOW A THREAT, NOT A PARTNER, FOR THE WEST.

PUTIN HAD TORN UP THE IDEA THAT EUROPE WOULD BE WHOLE, FREE, AND AT PEACE.

RRRIP

HE BECAME A PARIAH.

YET PUTIN COULDN'T RESIST FURTHER RAISING THE STAKES. HE FOMENTED A REBELLION IN EASTERN UKRAINE. HOWEVER, THAT OPERATION QUICKLY DESCENDED INTO CHAOS.

PUTIN HAD STOLEN DEFEAT FROM THE JAWS OF VICTORY.

RUSSIA'S INTELLIGENCE AGENCIES PULLED TOGETHER A MOTLEY CREW OF CRIMINALS, BIKER GANGS, AFGHAN WAR VETS...

...COSSACKS...

...AND EVEN RUSSIAN CIVIL WAR RE-ENACTORS TO DO THEIR DIRTY WORK. THAT TURNED OUT TO BE A REALLY BAD IDEA.

THE TAKEOVER OF EASTERN UKRAINE WAS CHAOTIC AND DISORGANIZED.

THE FSB AND GRU* BACKED DIFFERENT GROUPS OF MILITANTS, ENSNARING THEM IN TURF BATTLES.

IMAGES OF KREMLIN-SPONSORED LAWLESSNESS AND MAYHEM SHOCKED THE WORLD.

UKRAINIAN PRISONERS OF WAR WERE TORTURED AND SUMMARILY EXECUTED.

*THE GRU IS RUSSIA'S MILITARY INTELLIGENCE AGENCY.

EVEN WORSE, THE RUSSIANS STARTED GIVING THEIR PROXIES LOTS OF ADVANCED WEAPONS. RUSSIAN-LED SEPARATISTS MISTAKENLY SHOT DOWN A MALAYSIAN AIRLINES PASSENGER JET...

...KILLING 298 INNOCENT PEOPLE.

FOOTAGE OF PRO-RUSSIAN FIGHTERS LOOTING THE VICTIMS' BELONGINGS AT THE CRASH SITE SHOOK THE CONSCIENCES OF EUROPEAN GOVERNMENTS.

THEY FINALLY STOPPED DRAGGING THEIR FEET ABOUT U.S. REQUESTS FOR TOUGH ECONOMIC SANCTIONS.

NEARLY ALL DEALINGS WITH PUTIN AND HIS GOVERNMENT WERE CUT OFF.

THROUGHOUT THIS PERIOD, OBAMA AND OTHER LEADERS FOUND THEIR CONVERSATIONS WITH PUTIN MADDENING. HE REFUSED TO ADMIT THAT RUSSIA WAS INVOLVED IN ANY WAY IN THE CONFLICT.

ANGELA MERKEL TOLD OBAMA...

I'M NOT SURE PUTIN IS EVEN IN TOUCH WITH REALITY. IT'S LIKE HE'S IN ANOTHER WORLD.

A SENIOR WESTERN DIPLOMAT ONCE GAVE ME THE BEST EXPLANATION I'VE EVER HEARD ABOUT WHAT IT'S LIKE TO DEAL WITH PUTIN.

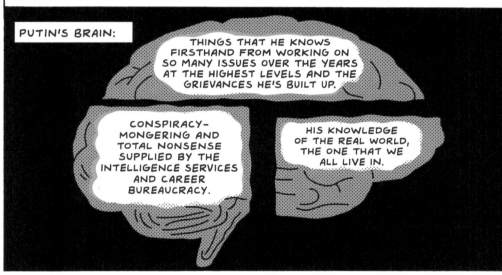

PUTIN'S BRAIN:

THINGS THAT HE KNOWS FIRSTHAND FROM WORKING ON SO MANY ISSUES OVER THE YEARS AT THE HIGHEST LEVELS AND THE GRIEVANCES HE'S BUILT UP.

CONSPIRACY-MONGERING AND TOTAL NONSENSE SUPPLIED BY THE INTELLIGENCE SERVICES AND CAREER BUREAUCRACY.

HIS KNOWLEDGE OF THE REAL WORLD, THE ONE THAT WE ALL LIVE IN.

THE PROBLEM WHEN YOU'RE TALKING TO HIM IS YOU NEVER KNOW WHICH PART OF HIS BRAIN HE'S OPERATING IN. HE CONSTANTLY TOGGLES BACK AND FORTH.

ONCE AGAIN, THE OBAMA ADMINISTRATION AND NATO WERE NOT INTERESTED IN A DIRECT MILITARY CONFRONTATION WITH THE KREMLIN. THEY TOLD THE UKRAINIANS TO SUE FOR PEACE.

WE ARE NOT GOING TO BE GETTING INTO A MILITARY EXCURSION IN UKRAINE.

IF THERE IS SOMEBODY IN D.C. THAT WOULD CLAIM THAT WE WOULD CONSIDER GOING TO WAR WITH RUSSIA OVER CRIMEA AND EASTERN UKRAINE...

...THEY SHOULD SPEAK UP AND BE VERY CLEAR ABOUT IT.

UKRAINE IS AN EXAMPLE OF WHERE WE HAVE TO BE VERY CLEAR ABOUT WHAT OUR CORE INTERESTS ARE AND WHAT WE ARE WILLING TO GO TO WAR FOR.

THE KREMLIN LEARNED AN IMPORTANT LESSON FROM THIS RESPONSE: WHEN RUSSIA ACTS RECKLESSLY OR ESCALATES MATTERS, THE WEST GETS REALLY SCARED.

NO ONE WANTS TO TANGLE WITH A NUCLEAR POWER THAT ACTS THIS WAY.

CHAPTER
6
FEET OF CLAY

THE HISTORY OF THE COLD WAR IS LITTERED WITH FAILED KGB ATTEMPTS TO TILT ELECTIONS AND DISRUPT POLITICAL LIFE IN THE U.S. AND OTHER COUNTRIES.

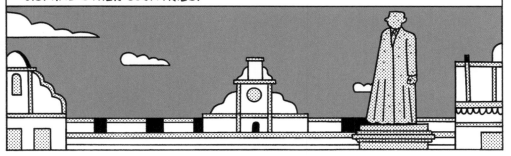

THE KGB PLANTED STORIES AROUND THE WORLD. THEY GOT JOURNALISTS TO WRITE THAT PENTAGON SCIENTISTS SECRETLY CREATED HIV, THE VIRUS THAT CAUSES AIDS.

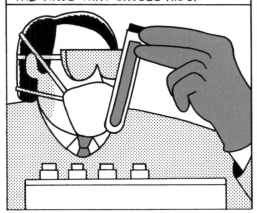

IN THE 1980S, THE KGB TRIED TO PUSH AN UNFRIENDLY GERMAN GOVERNMENT OUT OF POWER AND MANIPULATED THE ANTI-NUCLEAR MOVEMENT.

DURING THE 1984 U.S. PRESIDENTIAL ELECTION, KGB OFFICERS PROMOTED THE SLOGAN:

REAGAN MEANS WAR

NO ONE NOTICED. REAGAN WON IN A LANDSLIDE.

THE KGB CREATED A WHISPER CAMPAIGN TO SPREAD RUMORS THAT FBI DIRECTOR J. EDGAR HOOVER AND LEADING ANTI-COMMUNIST SENATOR HENRY "SCOOP" JACKSON WERE SECRETLY GAY.

IN 2017, THE RUSSIANS PUSHED SIMILAR STORIES ABOUT FRENCH PRESIDENT EMMANUEL MACRON.

UKRAINE BECAME A KEY TESTING GROUND FOR HARD-EDGED RUSSIAN POLITICAL TRENCH WARFARE.

RUSSIA LAUNCHED PRESSURE CAMPAIGNS AND INFLUENCE OPERATIONS TO BREAK UKRAINIANS' WILL TO FIGHT.

MANY OF THEM WERE RECYCLED AND REPURPOSED DURING THE 2016 U.S. PRESIDENTIAL ELECTION.

WELL BEFORE AMERICANS STARTED EDUCATING THEMSELVES ABOUT TERMS LIKE *ACTIVE MEASURES*, *DISINFORMATION*, AND *CYBERATTACK*...

...THE PEOPLE OF UKRAINE WERE UNDER ASSAULT FROM SUCH TACTICS 24/7.

THE PARALLELS ARE UNMISTAKABLE. FOR EXAMPLE, LEAKS OF EMBARRASSING INFORMATION.

UKRAINE, FEBRUARY 2014: TAPE OF THE TOP U.S. DIPLOMATS WORKING ON THE UKRAINE CRISIS POSTED ON YOUTUBE

U.S. STATE DEPT. : "F*CK THE E.U."

"F*CK THE EU!" (ORIGINAL FILE) AMB. NULAND AND AMB. PYATT

46K views years ago

👍 195   👎 16   ↷ Share   ↓ Download   ⊞ Save

🔍 FreiBILDfuerAlle
9K SUBSCRIBERS   SUBSCRIBE

COMMENTS   ↕

U.S., 2016: RELEASE OF HACKED DNC EMAILS ATTACKING BERNIE SANDERS ON THE EVE OF THE DEMOCRATIC NATIONAL CONVENTION

PHILADELPHIA
4:45 EST

BREAKING NEWS
HACKED DNC EMAILS ROCK U.S.
TONIGHT: BERNIE SANDERS
MICHELLE OBAMA   cnn

UKRAINE, MARCH 2014: TAPE OF FORMER UKRAINIAN PRIME MINISTER TYMOSHENKO

"[I]t's time we grab our guns and go kill those damn Russians together with their leader. I am ready to grab a machine gun and shoot that motherf--ker [Putin] in the head." —Tymoshenko

RT

U.S., 2016: WIKILEAKS RELEASE OF EMAILS STOLEN BY RUSSIAN MILITARY HACKERS FROM HILLARY CLINTON'S INNER CIRCLE. TRUMP USED THEM TO PAINT CLINTON AS SLEAZY AND UNETHICAL.

WIKILEAKS, I LOVE WIKILEAKS. THIS WIKILEAKS STUFF IS UNBELIEVABLE. IT TELLS YOU THE INNER HEART, YOU GOTTA READ IT. THIS WIKILEAKS IS LIKE A TREASURE TROVE.

TRUMP
PENCE

UKRAINE 2014: RUSSIAN TROLLS AND STATE MEDIA TRIED TO INFLAME DEBATE ABOUT THE UKRAINE CRISIS. THEY PUSHED THE KREMLIN'S CLAIMS THAT THE REVOLUTION WAS A CIA-BACKED COUP D'ETAT LED BY NEO-NAZIS AND ULTRA-NATIONALISTS.

THEY COULD HAVE AT LEAST CALLED US!...NOT A WORD!

ON THE CONTRARY, THERE WAS FULL SUPPORT OF THOSE WHO COMMITTED THIS COUP. THIS IS WHAT THEY DID WITH THEIR OWN HANDS.

THIS WAS THE FIRST TIME WHEN THE CHEATING WAS DONE SO RUDELY AND INSOLENTLY.

LIVE RT | PUTIN: CIA AND NAZIS IN UKRAINE | MOSCOW

U.S., 2016: THE INTERNET RESEARCH AGENCY BOMBARDED SOCIAL MEDIA PLATFORMS, SEEKING TO DEEPEN U.S. POLITICAL AND SOCIAL DIVISIONS. DURING THE 2016 CAMPAIGN, THESE POSTS REACHED MILLIONS OF AMERICANS.

 ARMY OF JESUS   👍 LIKE PAGE

1.7 MILLION LIKES 435,123 SHARES

👍 LIKE   💬 COMMENTS   ➤ SHARE

THERE WAS SERIOUS ELECTION INTERFERENCE IN BOTH COUNTRIES.

UKRAINE, MAY 2014: RUSSIAN HACKERS NEARLY DERAILED THE UKRAINIAN PRESIDENTIAL ELECTIONS BY ATTACKING THE MAIN ONLINE VOTE TALLYING MACHINERY.

ON ELECTION DAY, RUSSIAN STATE TV TRIED TO UNDERMINE CONFIDENCE IN THE RESULT WITH A FAKE CHART...

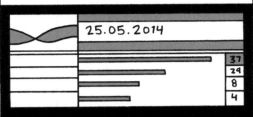

25.05.2014

37
29
8
4

...SHOWING THAT A NOTORIOUS NEO-NAZI HAD TRIUMPHED UNEXPECTEDLY.

U.S., 2016: ACCORDING TO THE MUELLER REPORT, RUSSIAN GOVERNMENT HACKERS ATTACKED "U.S. STATE AND LOCAL ELECTION ENTITIES, SUCH AS..."

"...STATE BOARDS OF ELECTIONS..."

STATE OF ILLINOIS GOVERNMENT OFFICE

"...SECRETARIES OF STATE, AND COUNTY GOVERNMENTS..."

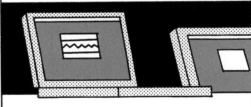

"...INDIVIDUALS WHO WORKED FOR THOSE ENTITIES..."

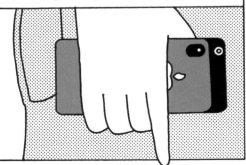

"...AND VOTING TECHNOLOGY COMPANIES."

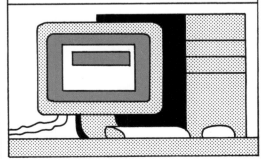

MOSCOW LAUNCHED AGGRESSIVE HACKING OPERATIONS.

U.S., 2014—2015: RUSSIAN INTELLIGENCE PENETRATED THE EMAIL SYSTEM OF THE WHITE HOUSE, STATE DEPARTMENT, AND PENTAGON...

...AND ACCESSED SOME OF OBAMA'S PERSONAL CORRESPONDENCE.

RE:

Barack Obama: <bho679@wh.gov>
To: Joe Biden: <jb025@wh.gov>

Joe, we need a serious conversatio about this issue. I don't see it the same way.

UKRAINE: HACKERS WORKING FOR RUSSIAN INTELLIGENCE CONDUCTED THOUSANDS OF ATTACKS AGAINST THE GOVERNMENT, BANKS, BUSINESSES, NGOS, AND OTHER TARGETS.

DECEMBER 2015: THE GRU STAGED THE FIRST KNOWN CYBERATTACK THAT CAUSED POWER OUTAGES.

DECEMBER 2016: HACKERS TURNED OUT THE LIGHTS IN CENTRAL KYIV.

IN JUNE 2017, RUSSIAN MILITARY INTELLIGENCE LAUNCHED "THE MOST DESTRUCTIVE AND COSTLY CYBER-ATTACK IN HISTORY" (NICKNAMED NOTPETYA). THE FAKE RANSOMWARE ATTACK PARALYZED THE UKRAINIAN ECONOMY BEFORE SPREADING AROUND THE WORLD.

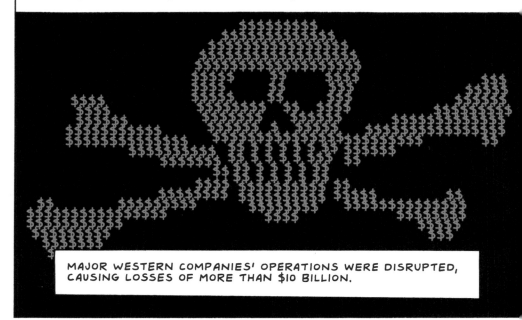

MAJOR WESTERN COMPANIES' OPERATIONS WERE DISRUPTED, CAUSING LOSSES OF MORE THAN $10 BILLION.

THE UKRAINE CRISIS TURNED PUTIN INTO A MORE INSULAR FIGURE. HE HAD LESS TIME FOR LONGTIME COLLEAGUES AND FRIENDS. HE RECRUITED YOUNGER PEOPLE GOOD AT FOLLOWING ORDERS.

PUTIN RELIED MORE AND MORE ON HIS OWN INTUITION.

THE KREMLIN'S CYBER OPERATIONS AND HACK-AND-LEAK ATTACKS ON WESTERN POLITICIANS TOOK PEOPLE BY SURPRISE. BUT MANY OF THESE ACTIVITIES WERE CONSISTENT WITH A PLAYBOOK DATING BACK TO THE SOVIET ERA.

ACCORDING TO GENERAL KALUGIN, PUTIN'S BOSS FROM HIS LENINGRAD KGB DAYS, THE KGB'S TOP MISSION WAS...

...NOT INTELLIGENCE COLLECTION, BUT SUBVERSION— ACTIVE MEASURES TO WEAKEN THE WEST, TO DRIVE WEDGES IN THE WESTERN COMMUNITY ALLIANCES OF ALL SORTS, PARTICULARLY NATO.

TO SOW DISCORD AMONG ALLIES, TO WEAKEN THE UNITED STATES IN THE EYES OF THE PEOPLE OF EUROPE, ASIA, AFRICA, LATIN AMERICA...

AND THUS TO PREPARE GROUND IN CASE WAR REALLY OCCURS.

STILL, PUTIN FELT LONELY, DESPITE THE FACT THAT CZAR ALEXANDER III HAD FAMOUSLY DECLARED, "RUSSIA ONLY HAS TWO ALLIES: ITS ARMY AND NAVY."

SO HE STARTED BUYING SOME FRIENDS. THE EASIEST PICKINGS WERE ON THE FRINGES OF EUROPEAN AND U.S. POLITICS.

A CONSERVATIVE RUSSIAN OLIGARCH NAMED KONSTANTIN MALOFEYEV, WITH TIES TO THE FSB AND RUSSIAN ORTHODOX CHURCH...

...SET UP A SECRET MEETING IN VIENNA FOR NATIONALIST, FAR-RIGHT, AND MONARCHIST FIGURES FROM FRANCE, SPAIN, AUSTRIA, AND OTHER COUNTRIES.

BEFORE TOO LONG, FAR-RIGHT POLITICIANS AND ACTIVISTS FROM EUROPE WERE PARADED AROUND RUSSIAN-CONTROLLED CRIMEA AND DONBAS.

THE RUSSIAN PROPAGANDA APPARATUS ALSO HAD A KEY ROLE TO PLAY. FOR YEARS, IT HAD BEEN PUMPING OUT HOURS OF INTERVIEWS IN ENGLISH WITH FRINGE VOICES LIKE BREXIT MASTERMIND NIGEL FARAGE...

RT

...INFOWARS'S ALEX JONES...

RT ALEX JONES
INFOWARS.COM

...AND ALT-RIGHT IDEOLOGUE RICHARD SPENCER.

RT RICHARD SPENCER
WHITE SUPREMACIST

THEY HAMMERED THE WEST...

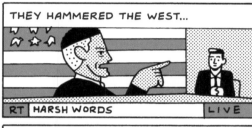

RT HARSH WORDS   LIVE

...FAWNED OVER PUTIN...

RT PUTIN'S STRENGTH   LIVE

...ENDORSED RUSSIAN MOVES IN UKRAINE...

RT UKRAINE ULTRANATIONALISTS

...AND ATTACKED PERENNIAL KREMLIN ENEMIES LIKE GEORGE SOROS.

RT BILLIONAIRE'S HIDDEN HAND

RUSSIA ALSO FILLED THE COFFERS OF POPULIST, NATIONALIST, AND FAR-RIGHT POLITICAL PARTIES, INCLUDING MARINE LE PEN'S NATIONAL FRONT...

...WHICH GOT A SWEETHEART LOAN FROM A SHADOWY RUSSIAN BANK.

ALL OF THIS WAS ALSO IN KEEPING WITH WELL-ESTABLISHED SOVIET-ERA PRACTICES. IN THE IMMEDIATE WAKE OF THE OCTOBER REVOLUTION...

...THE KREMLIN'S OPERATIVES HAD ASSEMBLED NETWORKS OF FRONT ORGANIZATIONS, AGENTS OF INFLUENCE, AND POLITICAL PARTIES THAT TOED MOSCOW'S LINE.

ANTI-COMMUNISTS IN THE U.S. HAD A HARSH NAME FOR THESE FELLOW TRAVELERS: "USEFUL IDIOTS."

THE KREMLIN'S SUBVERSIVE ACTIVITIES WERE DRAMATICALLY SCALED BACK WHEN THE SOVIET UNION COLLAPSED.

BUT SOME SHADOWY INTELLECTUALS WITH TIES TO RUSSIAN SECURITY AGENCIES AND THE MILITARY BUILT BRIDGES TO EUROPEAN RADICAL AND FASCIST GROUPS.

RIGHT AFTER THE SOVIET COLLAPSE, A HOMEGROWN, WILD-EYED FASCIST WRITER (COMPLETE WITH REQUISITE LONG BEARD AND TIES TO RUSSIAN INTELLIGENCE SERVICES) NAMED ALEXANDER DUGIN ARRANGED SPEAKING TOURS AT THE RUSSIAN ARMY GENERAL STAFF ACADEMY FOR FRENCH FAR-RIGHT THINKERS.

ALAIN DE BENOIST

DUGIN LATER HELPED ORGANIZE THE SECRET MEETING WITH EUROPEAN NATIONALIST POLITICIANS IN VIENNA.

REMEMBER PUTIN'S EMBRACE OF FAMILY VALUES AND ATTACKS ON SAME-SEX MARRIAGE DURING THE PUSSY RIOT SCANDAL? THAT HELPED ATTRACT SUPPORT FROM U.S. SOCIAL CONSERVATIVES...

...LIKE FRANKLIN GRAHAM, SON OF FAMED EVANGELIST BILLY GRAHAM.

MANY CHURCHES IN AMERICA HAVE STARTED TO SUPPORT HOMOSEXUALITY. THIS IS TERRIBLE. IT'S A SIN AND IT'S AGAINST GOD.

I CALL FOR PRAYERS FOR THE PRESIDENT OF RUSSIA, WHO IS PROTECTING TRADITIONAL CHRISTIANITY.

IN JUNE 2013, STEVE KING, A REPUBLICAN WHITE NATIONALIST MEMBER OF CONGRESS FROM IOWA, VISITED MOSCOW...

...WITH PUTIN BUDDY (AND FORMER ACTION MOVIE STAR) STEVEN SEAGAL. WHILE HE WAS IN MOSCOW, KING SLAMMED PUSSY RIOT.

FUTURE SENIOR ADVISORS FOR TRUMP'S PRESIDENTIAL CAMPAIGN AND HIS WHITE HOUSE TEAM EXTENDED OLIVE BRANCHES TO THE KREMLIN. IN 2014, STEVE BANNON SAID:

WE, THE JUDEO–CHRISTIAN WEST, REALLY HAVE TO LOOK AT WHAT PUTIN'S TALKING ABOUT AS FAR AS TRADITIONALISM GOES.

TRUMP'S FIRST NATIONAL SECURITY ADVISER, LT. GEN. MICHAEL FLYNN, ACCEPTED $45,000 IN 2015 TO ATTEND A GALA DINNER IN MOSCOW TO CELEBRATE THE KREMLIN'S PROPAGANDA NETWORK, RUSSIA TODAY (RT).

HE WAS SEATED NEXT TO PUTIN.

MEANWHILE, ALEKSANDR TORSHIN, THE INVESTIGATOR OF THE BESLAN MASSACRE, HAD BEEN BUILDING BRIDGES TO THE NATIONAL RIFLE ASSOCIATION (NRA) AND GOP/CONSERVATIVE CIRCLES.

SOMEHOW THAT DIDN'T RAISE RED FLAGS FOR THE AMERICANS HE CULTIVATED.

HE ARRANGED SPLASHY TRIPS TO MOSCOW FOR PROMINENT GOP ACTIVISTS LIKE FOX NEWS COMMENTATOR SHERIFF DAVID CLARKE.

DAVID A. CLARKE, JR. @SHERIFFCLARKE | FOLLOW

RETWEETS 1,227   LIKES 915

ON TORSHIN'S FREQUENT VISITS TO THE U.S. HE WAS ACCOMPANIED BY 20-SOMETHING MARIA BUTINA, WHO CLAIMED TO RUN A GUN RIGHTS ORGANIZATION BUT WAS SECRETLY HELPING THE RUSSIAN GOVERNMENT.

BEFORE TOO LONG, SHE WAS LIVING WITH A REPUBLICAN APPARATCHIK WHO HELPED HER WORM HER WAY INTO PROMINENT GOP CIRCLES.

ONE OF TRUMP'S TOP NATIONAL SECURITY AIDES TOOK HER TO A STYX CONCERT ON THE EVE OF THE 2016 ELECTION.

I ENCOUNTERED TORSHIN AND BUTINA WHEN HE GAVE A CLOSED-DOOR TALK AT A D.C. THINK-TANK EVENT IN 2015. HE DEMONSTRATED ZERO EXPERTISE IN THE ADVERTISED TOPIC, MONETARY POLICY.

THEY SAID THEY WERE ON THEIR WAY TO THE NRA CONVENTION IN NASHVILLE.

THE WHOLE THING WAS PRETTY WEIRD.

DURING THE 2016 CAMPAIGN, TORSHIN AND BUTINA MANAGED TO MEET WITH DONALD TRUMP JR. AND WISCONSIN GOVERNOR SCOTT WALKER, A GOP PRESIDENTIAL ASPIRANT.

A COURT FILING BY A SENIOR FBI COUNTER-INTELLIGENCE OFFICIAL STATES...

"RUSSIAN INTELLIGENCE SERVICES WILL BE ABLE TO USE BUTINA'S INFORMATION FOR YEARS TO COME..."

"...IN THEIR EFFORTS TO SPOT AND ASSESS AMERICANS WHO MAY BE SUSCEPTIBLE TO RECRUITMENT AS FOREIGN INTELLIGENCE ASSETS."

MEANWHILE, THE RUSSIAN GOVERNMENT WAS FINDING OTHER WAYS TO DRAIN SUPPORT FROM THE POLITICAL MAINSTREAM AND TO SUPPORT FRINGE FIGURES LIKE...

...WIKILEAKS'S JULIAN ASSANGE...

...AND THE U.S. GREEN PARTY'S JILL STEIN, WHO RAN FOR PRESIDENT IN 2016.

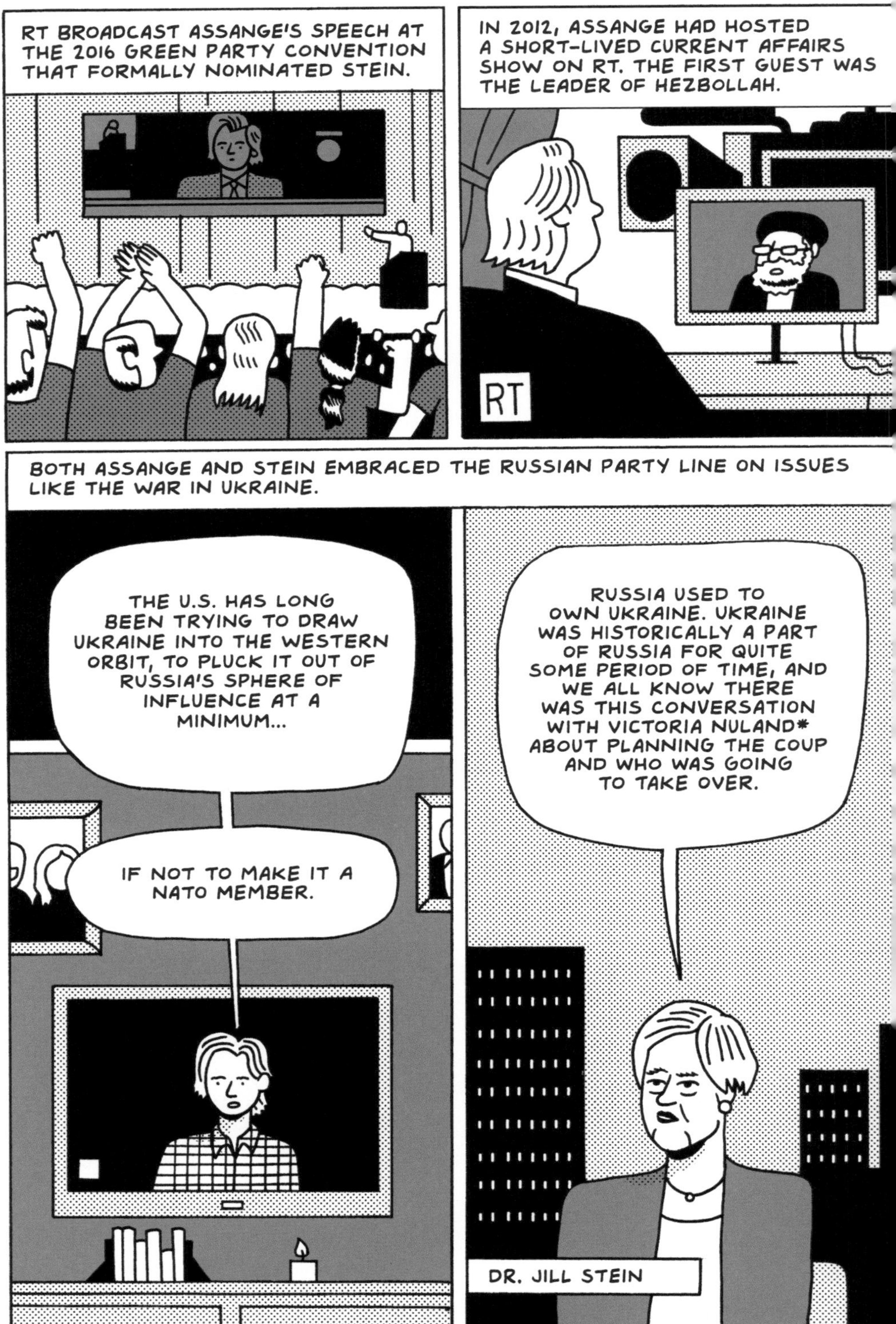
RT BROADCAST ASSANGE'S SPEECH AT THE 2016 GREEN PARTY CONVENTION THAT FORMALLY NOMINATED STEIN.
IN 2012, ASSANGE HAD HOSTED A SHORT-LIVED CURRENT AFFAIRS SHOW ON RT. THE FIRST GUEST WAS THE LEADER OF HEZBOLLAH.
RT
BOTH ASSANGE AND STEIN EMBRACED THE RUSSIAN PARTY LINE ON ISSUES LIKE THE WAR IN UKRAINE.
THE U.S. HAS LONG BEEN TRYING TO DRAW UKRAINE INTO THE WESTERN ORBIT, TO PLUCK IT OUT OF RUSSIA'S SPHERE OF INFLUENCE AT A MINIMUM...
IF NOT TO MAKE IT A NATO MEMBER.
RUSSIA USED TO OWN UKRAINE. UKRAINE WAS HISTORICALLY A PART OF RUSSIA FOR QUITE SOME PERIOD OF TIME, AND WE ALL KNOW THERE WAS THIS CONVERSATION WITH VICTORIA NULAND* ABOUT PLANNING THE COUP AND WHO WAS GOING TO TAKE OVER.
DR. JILL STEIN

*ASSISTANT SECRETARY OF STATE FOR EUROPEAN AFFAIRS

WE SHOULD ENCOURAGE UKRAINE TO BE NEUTRAL—WE HELPED FOMENT A COUP AGAINST A DEMOCRATICALLY ELECTED GOVERNMENT, WHERE ULTRA-NATIONALISTS AND EX-NAZIS THEN CAME TO POWER...

THE HOSTILE FACE-OFF WITH RUSSIA CAUSES THAT AND IS ENTIRELY MISPLACED—

LED BY WAR HAWKS IN THE OBAMA ADMINISTRATION—ESPECIALLY VICTORIA NULAND, WHO CHEERED ON AN OVERTHROW IN UKRAINE.

SEAN HANNITY INTERVIEW WITH ASSANGE, JANUARY 2017

CAN YOU SAY TO THE AMERICAN PEOPLE UNEQUIVOCALLY THAT YOU DID NOT GET THIS INFORMATION ABOUT THE DNC, JOHN PODESTA'S EMAILS—CAN YOU TELL THE AMERICAN PEOPLE ONE THOUSAND PERCENT YOU DID NOT GET IT FROM RUSSIA?

FOX

YES.

OR ANYBODY ASSOCIATED WITH RUSSIA?

WE CAN SAY AND WE HAVE SAID REPEATEDLY OVER THE LAST TWO MONTHS...

...THAT OUR SOURCE IS NOT THE RUSSIAN GOVERNMENT AND IT IS NOT A STATE PARTY.*

*IN REALITY, RUSSIAN GRU HACKERS GAVE WIKILEAKS THE DOCUMENTS THEY HAD STOLEN FROM THE DNC AND THE HILLARY CLINTON CAMPAIGN. (SOURCE: MUELLER REPORT)

JILL STEIN ATTENDED THE 2015 RT BIRTHDAY GALA DINNER AND SAT AT THE SAME HEAD TABLE WITH PUTIN AND MIKE FLYNN.

JILL STEIN'S VOTE TOTALS IN THE THREE STATES THAT DECIDED THE 2016 ELECTION (MICHIGAN, PENNSYLVANIA, AND WISCONSIN) WERE BIGGER THAN TRUMP'S MARGIN OF VICTORY IN EACH.

THE SUCCESS OF THESE HAPHAZARD, SOMETIMES QUIXOTIC, RUSSIAN EFFORTS WAS HARDLY FOREORDAINED.

DID ANYONE IN MOSCOW SERIOUSLY BELIEVE THAT INSURGENT POLITICIANS LIKE DONALD TRUMP OR THE U.K.'S NIGEL FARAGE WOULD SOMEDAY BE RUNNING THE SHOW IN WASHINGTON AND LONDON? I DOUBT IT.

THE KREMLIN AND ITS PROXIES DIDN'T CREATE AMERICA'S INTENSE POLITICAL POLARIZATION...

...OR THE POWER OF SOCIAL MEDIA.

RATHER, THEY ARE EXPLOITING AND AMPLIFYING EXISTING VULNERABILITIES, TAKING ADVANTAGE OF THEM FOR MOSCOW'S OWN PURPOSES.

AS AN OPEN SOCIETY, THE WEST'S PROBLEMS ARE ON CONSTANT DISPLAY.

THE RUSSIANS ROUTINELY DO THEIR HOMEWORK AND GET A PRETTY GOOD HANDLE ON OUR WEAKNESSES AND SORE POINTS.

THE KREMLIN DIDN'T NEED THOUSANDS OF SPIES TO TELL THEM THAT AMERICANS IN 2016 WERE FED UP WITH BUSINESS AS USUAL.

OR THAT THE 2008 GLOBAL FINANCIAL CRISIS HAD UNLEASHED HUGE WAVES OF POPULAR ANGER AND ANTI-ELITE SENTIMENT.

OR THAT OUR TWO-PARTY SYSTEM IS IN DEEP CRISIS.

THE MIDDLE CLASS IN THE U.S. HAS NOT BENEFITED FROM GLOBALIZATION; IT WAS LEFT OUT WHEN THIS PIE WAS DIVIDED UP.

THE TRUMP TEAM SENSED THIS VERY KEENLY AND CLEARLY, AND THEY USED THIS IN THE ELECTION CAMPAIGN.

IT IS WHERE YOU SHOULD LOOK FOR REASONS BEHIND TRUMP'S VICTORY...

...RATHER THAN IN ANY ALLEGED FOREIGN INTERFERENCE.

LIKE THE HIJACKERS ON 9/11, SOME OF THE WEAPONS THAT MOSCOW RELIED ON WERE CHEAP. BUT THEY COULD CAUSE SPECTACULAR HARM.

AND JUST LIKE 9/11, RUSSIAN INTERFERENCE IN THE 2016 ELECTION SUCCEEDED BEYOND THE KREMLIN'S WILDEST DREAMS.

ON ONE LEVEL, THE KREMLIN'S PLAN LOOKED SLOPPY— IT RELIED HEAVILY ON HUCKSTERS AND GRIFTERS. BUT ON ANOTHER LEVEL, THIS STRATEGY WORKED TO THEIR ADVANTAGE.

IT GAVE THE KREMLIN PLAUSIBLE DENIABILITY.

ONE LONGTIME KREMLIN OBSERVER EXPLAINED THAT PEOPLE AT THE HIGHEST LEVELS IN THE KREMLIN OFTEN RELY ON HINTS AND NODS, INSTEAD OF DIRECT COMMANDS.

"THEY NEVER SAY CLEARLY SOMETHING OUTRAGEOUS LIKE, 'PLEASE MURDER THOSE PEOPLE,' OR..."

PLEASE STEAL THOSE BILLIONS OF DOLLARS.

"THAT'S IMPOSSIBLE. THEY USUALLY SAY..."

DO WHAT YOU HAVE TO DO. YOU KNOW WHAT YOU'RE SUPPOSED TO DO, SO PLEASE GO AHEAD.

KREMLIN ALLIES LIKE THE OWNER OF THE INTERNET RESEARCH AGENCY OPERATE ON A SIMPLE PREMISE: BY DOING THE THINGS THAT YOU THINK PUTIN WANTS, YOU HAVE A BETTER CHANCE OF GETTING MORE PRIVILEGES AND FINANCIAL BENEFITS FROM THE KREMLIN.

IT'S A CONVENIENT ARRANGEMENT: THE KREMLIN GETS CAPABILITIES TO CONDUCT OFF-THE-BOOKS OPERATIONS THAT IT DOESN'T HAVE TO PAY FOR...

...AND CAN DISSOCIATE ITSELF WHENEVER THINGS GET STICKY.

EITHER WAY, TRUMP WAS USEFUL FOR A KREMLIN INTENT ON DISCREDITING THE U.S. ROLE IN THE WORLD.

AS FORMER CIA DIRECTOR MICHAEL HAYDEN PUT IT:

RUSSIA'S BACKING FOR TRUMP IS, WITHOUT QUESTION, THE MOST SUCCESSFUL COVERT INFLUENCE OPERATION IN RECORDED HISTORY.

CANDIDATE TRUMP'S BEHAVIOR CREATED A COUNTERINTELLIGENCE NIGHTMARE FOR OBAMA'S NATIONAL SECURITY TEAM.

TRUMP HELD SECRET TALKS DURING THE CAMPAIGN ABOUT A BIG REAL ESTATE DEAL IN RUSSIA—AND LIED ABOUT IT.

HE REPEATED KREMLIN TALKING POINTS ON ISSUES LIKE PUTIN, UKRAINE, NATO, AND SANCTIONS.

THE PEOPLE OF CRIMEA, FROM WHAT I'VE HEARD, WOULD RATHER BE WITH RUSSIA THAN WHERE THEY WERE.

ACCORDING TO INVESTIGATORS, TRUMP'S CAMPAIGN HAD 272 CONTACTS AND 38 MEETINGS WITH RUSSIAN GOVERNMENT-TIED REPRESENTATIVES AND CUT-OUTS.

HE REVELED IN RUSSIAN-BACKED DISINFORMATION AND HACKING OPERATIONS (E.G., WIKILEAKS).

DESPITE EXTENSIVE PRESS REPORTING ON RUSSIAN INTERFERENCE IN THE ELECTION, THE KREMLIN FORMALLY DENIED ANY INVOLVEMENT. YET BY SEPTEMBER 2016, PUTIN WAS CRACKING JOKES IN PUBLIC ABOUT THE HACKS.

ON THE DAY AFTER TRUMP'S ELECTION, RUSSIAN LAWMAKERS BROKE OUT THE CHAMPAGNE.

VIDEO SURFACED OF THE DUMA APPLAUDING THE ANNOUNCEMENT OF TRUMP'S VICTORY...

...AND OF PUTIN'S SPOKESMAN PESKOV LOOKING TOTALLY GIDDY IN NYC THE DAY AFTER THE ELECTION.

AS DETAILS ABOUT RUSSIA'S ROLE IN THE PRESIDENTIAL RACE QUICKLY LEAKED OUT, WASHINGTON PLUNGED INTO THE WORST POLITICAL CRISIS SINCE WATERGATE.

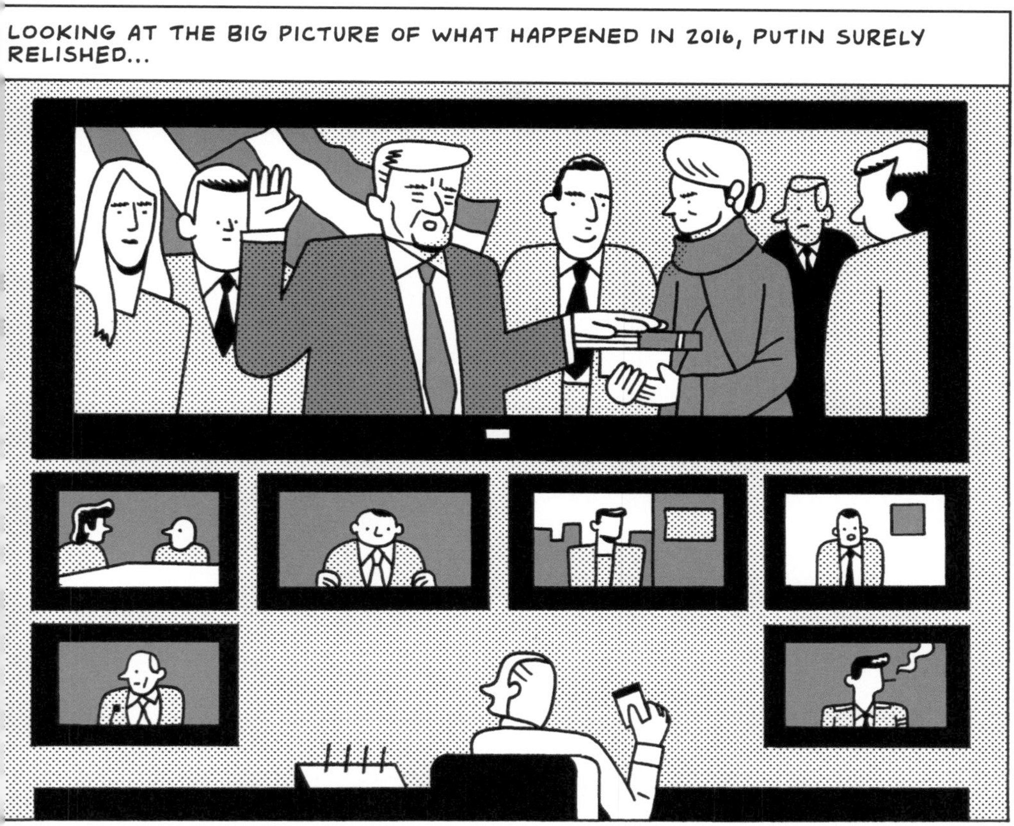
LOOKING AT THE BIG PICTURE OF WHAT HAPPENED IN 2016, PUTIN SURELY RELISHED...

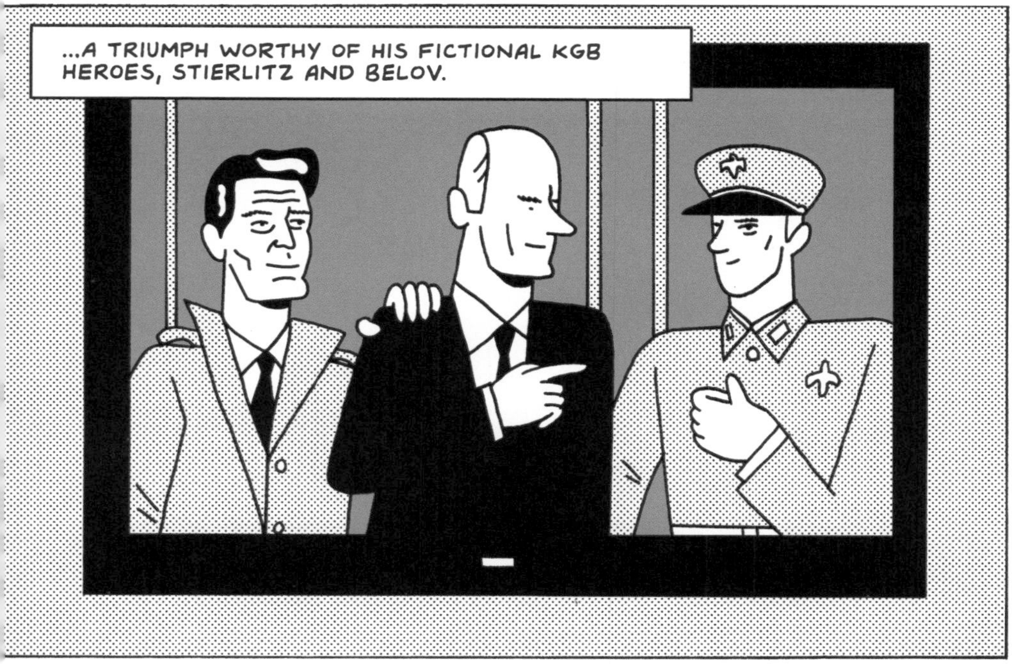
...A TRIUMPH WORTHY OF HIS FICTIONAL KGB HEROES, STIERLITZ AND BELOV.

BUT FOUR LONG YEARS OF TRUMP'S PRESIDENCY DIDN'T RESOLVE PUTIN'S SINGLE BIGGEST PIECE OF UNFINISHED BUSINESS: THE WAR IN UKRAINE.

ALTHOUGH RUSSIA'S MILITARY IS MUCH STRONGER THAN UKRAINE'S, PUTIN WAS UNABLE TO GET WHAT HE WANTED AT THE NEGOTIATING TABLE. THE STALEMATE IN DONBAS PREVENTED PUTIN FROM STRONG-ARMING KYIV INTO GIVING HIM CONTROL OVER UKRAINE'S MOST IMPORTANT DECISIONS.

PUTIN'S STRATEGY OF LOPPING OFF THE MOST HEAVILY PRO-RUSSIAN PARTS OF UKRAINE WAS FAR FROM BRILLIANT.

RUSSIA

UKRAINE

DONBAS

HIS ACTIONS MOTIVATED UKRAINE'S LEADERS TO BUILD EVEN CLOSER TIES WITH THE U.S., NATO, AND THE E.U.

CRIMEA

IN ONE SWOOP HE ALSO MADE UKRAINE'S LONG-DIVIDED POPULATION MORE UNIFIED AND WESTERN-ORIENTED.

PUTIN ALL BUT GUARANTEED THAT NO PRO-RUSSIAN FIGURE WOULD EVER FIND THE VOTES TO RULE THE COUNTRY EVER AGAIN.

БІЙ КОЛАБОРАНТАМ!

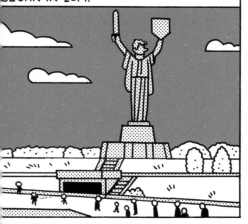

UKRAINE RECOVERED REMARKABLY WELL AFTER THE RUSSIAN ONSLAUGHT BEGAN IN 2014.

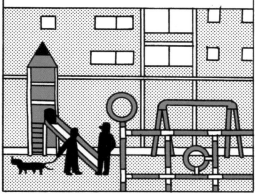

THE FIGHTING WAS LIMITED TO ONE REGION OF THE COUNTRY. BIG CITIES LIKE KYIV AND KHARKIV FLOURISHED.

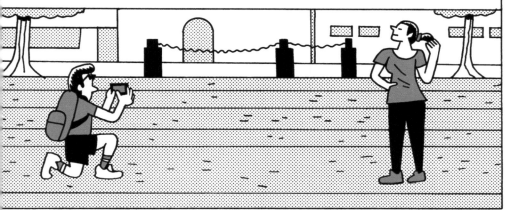

UKRAINIANS WERE EXTREMELY POOR AND THEIR GOVERNMENT WAS BADLY RUN, BUT THEY HAD AVOIDED THE WORST-CASE OUTCOME.

THE KREMLIN'S AGENTS OF INFLUENCE WERE EVERYWHERE. BUT PRO-RUSSIAN PARTIES NEVER ATTRACTED MUCH SUPPORT.

IN 2019, A COMEDIAN NAMED VOLODYMYR ZELENSKYY WON THE PRESIDENCY IN A LANDSLIDE. HE PROMISED TO END THE WAR AND FIGHT CORRUPTION.

U.S. AND E.U. LEADERS BECAME FRUSTRATED DURING ZELENSKYY'S FIRST YEARS IN OFFICE. THEY DOUBTED HIS READINESS TO PUSH OVERDUE REFORMS, BUT STILL TRIED TO BUILD CLOSER TIES.

PUTIN'S ANGER OVER UKRAINE MOUNTED. BACK IN 2013, THE WEST HAD SMILED POLITELY BUT TUNED HIM OUT.

SEND ANOTHER FORMAL COMPLAINT TO THE E.U.

EVERYONE THOUGHT THIS WAS JUST ANOTHER FLABBY EUROPEAN PROJECT. BUT ONCE A COUNTRY SIGNS UP, IT IS IN WEIGHT WATCHERS AND, IF THEY FOLLOW THE REGIMEN, THEY CHANGE. RUSSIA REALIZED THIS AND DID NOT LIKE IT.

FIONA HILL, TRUMP'S TOP RUSSIA ADVISER

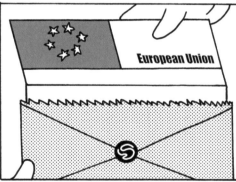

European Union

Dear President Putin,

Thank you for your interest in the European Union's foreign policy. Unfortunately, we are not taking any outside suggestions at the moment.

Best wishes
European Union

BACK IN 2014, THE WEST SLEEPWALKED INTO A CONFLICT WITH RUSSIA.

PUTIN HAD AN UNSHAKABLE DESIRE TO BRING UKRAINE BACK UNDER RUSSIA'S WING.

HE HATED UKRAINE'S DEMOCRACY.

UKRAINIANS ACTUALLY HAD THE RIGHT TO CHOOSE THEIR LEADERS IN FREE AND FAIR ELECTIONS.

VOTE HERE

HE TRIED TO PLANT SEEDS OF DIVISION BETWEEN EUROPE AND THE UNITED STATES.

THE KREMLIN ALSO ATTEMPTED TO UNDERMINE KEY COUNTRIES LIKE THE U.S., THE U.K., AND GERMANY FROM WITHIN SO THAT THEY BECAME LESS POTENT THREATS TO PUTIN'S REGIME.

HE ALSO LOOKED FOR WAYS TO CHANGE THE SUBJECT AND FORCE THE WEST TO DEAL WITH HIM ON HIS OWN TERMS.

RUSSIA'S STRATEGY WAS REMINISCENT OF HOW THE TALIBAN FOUGHT BACK AGAINST THE U.S. AFTER 9/11.

Dear America,

You have all the watches. But we have all the time.

Best wishes,
The Taliban

IT TOOK A WHILE FOR THE HUGE BLIND SPOTS IN PUTIN'S STRATEGY IN UKRAINE TO EMERGE.

THE DIRTY SECRET IS THAT PUTIN AND HIS TEAM IN THE KREMLIN LACK RUDIMENTARY KNOWLEDGE ABOUT UKRAINE. THEY STILL DON'T THINK THAT IT'S EVEN A REAL COUNTRY.

AS THE WAR GROUND ON, UKRAINE'S CITIZENS MADE HUGE SACRIFICES. THEY DOGGEDLY PROTECTED THEIR HARD-WON INDEPENDENCE FROM MOSCOW. THOUSANDS OF UKRAINIANS FROM ALL WALKS OF LIFE VOLUNTEERED TO FIGHT, PUTTING THEIR OWN LIVES ON THE LINE.

THE WEST INVESTED BIG MONEY IN HELPING TRAIN AND EQUIP WHAT WAS ONCE A RAGTAG ARMY.

ALL THE WHILE, PUTIN CONTINUED TO INSIST THAT...

...UKRAINIANS AND RUSSIANS ARE ACTUALLY ONE PEOPLE.

OLIVER STONE

IT'S A SELF-SERVING FANTASY.

PUTIN ISOLATED HIMSELF DURING THE COVID-19 PANDEMIC.

HE KEPT GETTING MORE AGITATED ABOUT UKRAINE. HE FRETTED THAT RUSSIA'S ENEMIES WERE "ABSORBING" THE COUNTRY INTO THE WEST.

HE STARTED PLANNING A SECRET MILITARY OPERATION TO TAKE OVER UKRAINE AND TO KILL ITS LEADERS.

THE RUSSIAN MILITARY COUNTED ON A SPEEDY VICTORY AND BEGAN ASSEMBLING A MASSIVE INVASION FORCE.

PUTIN RETREATED DEEPER INTO HIS BUNKER, LIMITING CONTACTS TO HIS INNER CIRCLE.

THEY GOT READY TO MOVE.

THEY SAW WESTERN LEADERS AS WEAKLINGS.

THEY WERE GEARING UP FOR A DECISIVE FIGHT AGAINST AMERICA, BUT IT WOULD TAKE PLACE ON RUSSIA'S DOORSTEP.

FOR YEARS PUTIN HAD MADE IT ABUNDANTLY CLEAR THAT UKRAINE WAS A NEURALGIC ISSUE FOR HIM.

VERY FEW WESTERN LEADERS RECOGNIZED THAT HE WAS DEAD SERIOUS ABOUT KEEPING NATO AND THE E.U. OUT OF RUSSIA'S BACKYARD.

HE'D FOUGHT A WAR IN GEORGIA IN 2008 FOR THESE VERY REASONS. BUT MEMORIES ARE SOMETIMES SHORT IN INTERNATIONAL AFFAIRS.

DINNER WITH PRESIDENT BUSH, 2008

YOU DON'T UNDERSTAND, GEORGE, THAT UKRAINE IS NOT EVEN A STATE. WHAT IS UKRAINE?

PART OF ITS TERRITORIES IS EASTERN EUROPE...

BUT THE GREATER PART IS A GIFT FROM US.

ONE-ON-ONE WITH U.S. AMBASSADOR

NO RUSSIAN LEADER COULD STAND IDLY BY IN THE FACE OF STEPS TOWARD NATO MEMBERSHIP FOR UKRAINE.

THAT WOULD BE A HOSTILE ACT TOWARD RUSSIA.

238

IN 2021, U.S. AND U.K. SPIES UNCOVERED PUTIN'S SECRET PLAN TO ATTACK UKRAINE. THE WHITE HOUSE LEAKED THE INFORMATION TO THROW PUTIN OFF-BALANCE.

THAT WAS A BIG CHANGE FROM 2014, WHEN OBAMA WAS BLINDSIDED BY PUTIN'S ACTIONS. HE HAD BEEN PREOCCUPIED WITH ISSUES LIKE THE IRAN NUCLEAR DEAL...

OBAMA CALLS IRAN'S PRES. | LIVE CNN

CLOUDY WITH a CHaNCe OF MEaTBaLLS WINS | NaS ♡ 31

...AND SECRET TALKS WITH CUBA ON REESTABLISHING DIPLOMATIC RELATIONS.

PRESIDENT BIDEN AND OTHER LEADERS RUSHED WEAPONS TO UKRAINE, HOPING TO SLOW THE RUSSIAN INVASION.

PUTIN AND HIS AIDES LIED SHAMELESSLY, DENYING THAT RUSSIA HAD ANY INTENTION OF INVADING UKRAINE. THE U.S. EVACUATED DIPLOMATS AND MILITARY ADVISERS JUST DAYS AHEAD OF THE RUSSIAN ASSAULT IN FEBRUARY 2022. UKRAINE WAS ALL ALONE.

THE BRAVERY OF BADLY OUTNUMBERED UKRAINIAN TROOPS AT THE BEGINNING OF THE WAR TRANSFIXED THE WORLD.

THEY REPELLED SOME EARLY RUSSIAN ATTACKS. AVERAGE CITIZENS TOOK UP ARMS OR TAUNTED THE INVADERS IN THE STREETS.

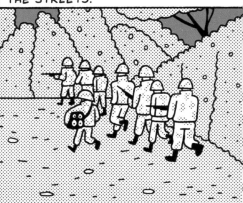

LIKE THE CORNERED RAT OF HIS CHILDHOOD, PUTIN CHOSE TO ESCALATE THE WAR TO FORCE UKRAINE TO BEND TO HIS WILL.

HE LAUNCHED ALL-OUT ASSAULTS ON UKRAINE'S BIGGEST CITIES.

INDISCRIMINATE RUSSIAN ATTACKS LED TO PANIC AND HUGE NUMBERS OF REFUGEES.

THE WORLD MOURNED.

AS RUSSIA ATTACKED MILITARY AND CIVILIAN TARGETS ACROSS UKRAINE, OTHER COUNTRIES LOOKED ON WITH HORROR.

PUTIN DID NOT REALIZE THAT HIS ATTACK WOULD SHAKE THE WORLD LIKE NO EVENT SINCE 9/11.

HE UNDERESTIMATED UKRAINIANS' RESOLVE.

HE ALSO UNDERESTIMATED THE UNITY OF THE WEST.

THANKS TO RUSSIA'S OIL AND GAS, PUTIN HAD COUNTED ON BUSINESS AS USUAL. INSTEAD, HE GOT UNPRECEDENTED SANCTIONS.

WHAT LAY AHEAD WAS ANYONE'S GUESS. WOULD PUTTING THE SCREWS TO PUTIN LEAD HIM TO BACK DOWN? OR TO DOUBLE DOWN?

CHAPTER
7
A DEEPLY UNSATISFYING ENDING

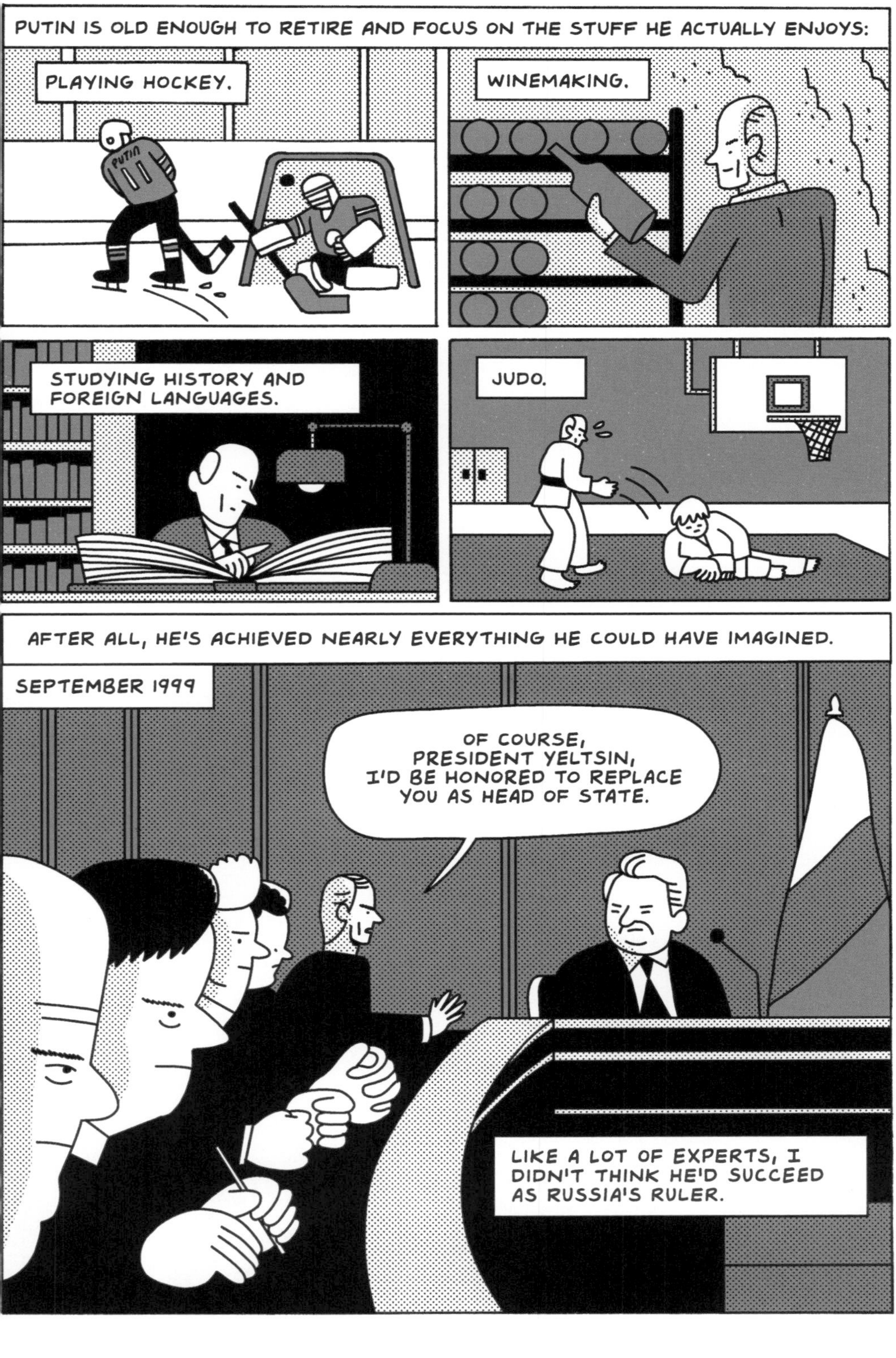
PUTIN IS OLD ENOUGH TO RETIRE AND FOCUS ON THE STUFF HE ACTUALLY ENJOYS:
PLAYING HOCKEY.
PUTIN
WINEMAKING.
STUDYING HISTORY AND FOREIGN LANGUAGES.
JUDO.
AFTER ALL, HE'S ACHIEVED NEARLY EVERYTHING HE COULD HAVE IMAGINED.
SEPTEMBER 1999
OF COURSE, PRESIDENT YELTSIN, I'D BE HONORED TO REPLACE YOU AS HEAD OF STATE.
LIKE A LOT OF EXPERTS, I DIDN'T THINK HE'D SUCCEED AS RUSSIA'S RULER.

OF COURSE, THAT WAS BEFORE HE'D HELPED DESTABILIZE THE UNITED STATES FROM WITHIN.

AND BEFORE AN UNABASHED PUTIN APOLOGIST HAD LANDED IN THE OVAL OFFICE.

BEFORE HE'D GONE TO WAR AGAINST HIS NEIGHBORS.

PUTIN COULD HAVE CALLED IT A DAY RIGHT AFTER TRUMP WAS ELECTED, WHEN HE WAS AT THE APEX OF HIS POWER AND WEALTH. WHY HAS HE KEPT ON GOING?

THE SHORT ANSWER IS, PUTIN IS STUCK. RUSSIA IS A COUNTRY WHERE NO ONE REALLY TRUSTS ANYBODY. GIVING UP POWER IS JUST TOO RISKY.

HE'S CORNERED HIMSELF— AND US.

IT MAY BE LONELY AT THE TOP, BUT GIVEN HOW RICKETY RUSSIA'S POLITICAL SYSTEM IS, PUTIN SLEEPS FAR MORE SOUNDLY INSIDE THE KREMLIN THAN HE WOULD OUTSIDE IT. THAT'S WHY HE'S SO DESPERATE TO STAY THERE.

FEAR IS HIS BEST FRIEND, SO HE MAKES IT CLEAR TO THE ELITE THAT ANY ACT OF DISLOYALTY CAN CARRY A HIGH PRICE.

U.S. SPY UNMASKED • MORE

BY CONVINCING AVERAGE RUSSIANS THAT THEY, TOO, LIVE IN A BESIEGED FORTRESS SURROUNDED BY ENEMIES, PUTIN CAN KEEP THEM ON HIS SIDE.

AND HE HAS MASTERED THE ART OF ANTAGONIZING MORE POWERFUL COUNTRIES LIKE THE UNITED STATES. WHEN THE U.S. HITS RUSSIA WITH SANCTIONS, PUTIN SPINS THE RESULTING ECONOMIC PAIN AS PROOF THAT RUSSIA IS UNDER ATTACK. IN THIS WAY, PUNISHING PUTIN CAN PARADOXICALLY HELP HIM.

THE SECRETIVE AND CONSPIRATORIAL NATURE OF PUTIN'S REGIME KEEPS US ALL GUESSING. IT'S WHY PEOPLE ARE ALWAYS ASKING THEMSELVES:

WHAT DOES PUTIN WANT?

AS THE HARVARD HISTORIAN EDWARD L. KEENAN WROTE, KREMLIN INSIDERS SINCE THE FOUNDING OF THE ROMANOV DYNASTY IN THE 17TH CENTURY HAVE LIVED BY A SIMPLE RULE:

DON'T CARRY RUBBISH OUT OF THE HUT.

"ONE DOES NOT REVEAL TO NON-PARTICIPANTS AUTHENTIC INFORMATION CONCERNING POLITICS, POLITICAL GROUPINGS, OR POINTS OF DISCORD."

ONE OF PUTIN'S ROLE MODELS, LEE KUAN YEW, THE FOUNDING FATHER OF MODERN SINGAPORE, LED HIS COUNTRY FOR SOME FIVE DECADES. HE WAS NINETY-ONE WHEN HE DIED.

PUTIN TURNS SEVENTY IN 2022. LOOKING TO LEE'S EXAMPLE, PUTIN MAY FIGURE THAT, HEALTH ALLOWING, HE HAS PLENTY OF TIME LEFT.

THINK ABOUT THAT FOR A SECOND.

SOMEBODY WHO WAS BORN IN 2000, WHEN PUTIN FIRST TOOK POWER, COULD EASILY BE INTO THEIR THIRTIES BY THE TIME HE LEAVES OFFICE.

STILL, WHETHER PUTIN'S REIGN ENDS A COUPLE OF YEARS OR A COUPLE OF DECADES FROM NOW, IT WILL END. IN THE MEANTIME, WE MUST RECKON WITH AN INCREASINGLY DANGEROUS SITUATION. HE WILL CONTINUE USING INTIMIDATION TACTICS AND THE THREAT OF UNCONTROLLED ESCALATION TO FORCE US TO BACK OFF.

CHALLENGING PUTIN HEAD-ON IS NOT AS EASY AS IT SOUNDS. YET EXAGGERATING PUTIN'S STRENGTH ALLOWS THE WEST TO IGNORE ITS OWN VULNERABILITIES—WHILE ALSO LOSING SIGHT OF RUSSIA'S. PUTIN PREYS ON OUR WEAKNESSES PRECISELY BECAUSE HIS COUNTRY CAN'T REALLY COMPETE WITH OURS MILITARILY, ECONOMICALLY, OR TECHNOLOGICALLY.

MAKE NO MISTAKE, THE WORLD DEFINITELY HAS A BIG RUSSIA PROBLEM TO CONFRONT.

BUT SEEING PUTIN AS HE WANTS US TO SEE HIM, RATHER THAN AS HE IS, ONLY MAKES THAT PROBLEM WORSE.

INTRODUCTION

Yaffa, Joshua. "Is Russian Meddling as Dangerous as We Think?" *New Yorker*. September 14, 2020. newyorker.com/magazine/2020/09/14/is-russian-meddling-as-dangerous -as-we-think.

CHAPTER 1

Adamovich, Ales, and Daniil Granin. *Leningrad Under Siege: First-Hand Accounts of the Ordeal*. Translated by Clare Burstall and Vladimir Kisselnikov. Barnsley, UK: Pen & Sword Military, 2007.

Gessen, Masha. *The Man Without a Face: The Unlikely Rise of Vladimir Putin*. New York: Riverhead Books, 2012.

Gevorkyan, Natalya, and Andrei Kolesnikov. "Zhelezniy Putin." *Kommersant*, March 10, 2000. kommersant.ru/doc/142144.

Gevorkyan, Natalya, Natalya Timakova, and Andrei Kolesnikov. *Ot Pervogo Litsa: Razgovory s Vladimirom Putinym*. Moscow: Vagrius, 2000.

Hoffman, David. "Putin's Career Rooted in Russia's KGB." *Washington Post*, January 30, 2000. washingtonpost.com/wp-srv/inatl/longterm/russiagov/putin.htm.

Kalugin, Oleg. *Spymaster: My Thirty-Two Years in Intelligence and Espionage Against the West*. New York: Basic Books, 2009.

Knight, Amy. "The Two Worlds of Vladimir Putin: The KGB." *Wilson Quarterly* 24 (Spring 2000): 32–37. archive.wilsonquarterly.com/sites/default/files/articles/WQ_VOL24 _SP_2000_Article_01_1.pdf.

Myers, Steven Lee. *The New Tsar: The Rise and Reign of Vladimir Putin*. New York: Vintage Books, 2015.

Neef, Christian. "A Complete Conformist." *Spiegel International*, October 20, 2003. spiegel.de/international/spiegel/espionage-a-complete-conformist-a-270555.html.

Nikitinskiy, Leonid, and Yuriy Shapkov. "Putin v Razvedke: 'Zavklubom ili Superagent.'" *Moskovskiye Novosti*, January 25, 2000.

Putin, Vladimir. "Zhizn' Takaya Prostaya Shutka i Zhestokaya." *Russkiy Pioner*, April 30, 2015. ruspioner.ru/cool/m/single/4655.

Rostovtsev, Aleksey. *Rezidentura: Ya Sluzhil Vmeste s Putinym*. Moscow: Algoritm, 2016.

Sarotte, Mary Elise. *The Collapse: The Accidental Opening of the Berlin Wall*. New York: Basic Books, 2014.

———. "Putin's View of Power Was Formed Watching East Germany Collapse." *Guardian* (US edition), October 1, 2014. theguardian.com/commentisfree/2014/oct/01/putin -power-east-germany-russia-kgb-dresden.

Sharogradskiy, Andrey. "Interv'yu s Byvshim Sosluzhivtsem Vladimira Putina." *Radio Svoboda*, November 11, 2003. svoboda.org/a/24187711.html.

Stasi Document (declassified). "Gewalteskalation am Dresdner Hauptbahnhof." stasi -unterlagen-archiv.de/informationen-zur-stasi/themen/beitrag/gewalteskalation-am -dresdener-hauptbahnhof/.

Stasi Document (declassified). "Schilderung der Ereignisse in Dresden zwischen dem 3. und 8. Oktober 1989 durch den Leiter der BVfs." stasi-mediathek.de/medien /schilderung-der-ereignisse-in-dresden-zwischen-dem-3-und-8-oktober-1989-durch -den-leiter-der-bvfs/blatt/1/.

CHAPTER 2

Bogatyrev, Sergei. "Kormlenie." Global Informality Project. in-formality.com/wiki/index .php?title=Kormlenie_(Pre-Soviet_Russia).

Burns, William J. *The Back Channel: A Memoir of American Diplomacy and the Case for Its Renewal*. New York: Random House, 2019.

———. "The Putin Files: William Burns." Interview by Michael Kirk. *Frontline*, June 14, 2017. pbs.org/wgbh/frontline/interview/william-burns/.

Hadley, Stephen J. "Stephen J. Hadley Oral History." George W. Bush Oral History Project, University of Virginia, Miller Center, October 31, 2011; November 1, 2011. millercenter.org /the-presidency/presidential-oral-histories/stephen-j-hadley-oral-history.

Hill, Fiona, and Clifford G. Gaddy. *Mr. Putin: Operative in the Kremlin*. Washington, DC: Brookings Institution Press, 2015.

Hosking, Geoffrey. *Russia and the Russians: A History*. Cambridge, MA: Harvard University Press, 2001.

Inozemtsev, Vladislav L. "Neo-Feudalism Explained." *American Interest* 6, no. 4 (March 1, 2011). the-american-interest.com/2011/03/01/neo-feudalism-explained/.

Kotkin, Stephen. "Defining Territories and Empires: from Mongol Ulus to Russian Siberia 1200–1800." In *Socio-Cultural Dimensions of the Changes in the Slavic-Eurasian World*. Sapporo: Hokkaido University Slavic Research Center, 1997. scholar.princeton.edu/sites/default/files/defining_territories_and_empires__from_mongol_ulus_to_russian_siberia1200_1800_0.pdf.

Ledeneva, Alena V. "Russia's Practical Norms and Informal Governance: The Origins of Endemic Corruption." In *Social Research* 80, no. 4 (Winter 2013). discovery.ucl.ac.uk/id/eprint/1421771/.

Müller, Martin. "After Sochi 2014: Costs and Impacts of Russia's Olympic Games." *Eurasian Geography and Economics* 55, no. 6 (2014): 628–55. tandfonline.com/doi/full/10.1080/15387216.2015.1040432.

Pipes, Richard. *Property and Freedom*. New York: Vintage Books, 2000.

Poe, Marshall. "Herberstein and Origin of the European Image of Muscovite Government." In *450 Jahre Sigismund von Herbersteins Rerum Moscoviticarum Commentarii: 1549–1999*, edited by Frank Kämpfer. Wiesbaden: Harrassowitz Verlag, 2001. iro.uiowa.edu/esploro/outputs/acceptedManuscript/Herberstein-and-Origin-of-the-European/9983557599802771.

Priess, David. *The President's Book of Secrets: The Untold Story of Intelligence Briefings to America's Presidents*. New York: Public Affairs, 2016.

Sestanovich, Stephen. "Could It Have Been Otherwise?" *American Interest* 10, no. 5 (April 14, 2015). the-american-interest.com/2015/04/14/could-it-have-been-otherwise/.

U.S. Department of Justice, Office of the Inspector General. "Review of Four FISA Applications and Other Aspects of the FBI's Crossfire Hurricane Investigation." December 2019. int.nyt.com/data/documenthelper/6565-doj-inspector-general-horowitz-report/8125be3a81c0d37f40d9/optimized/full.pdf#page=1.

CHAPTER 3

Baker, Peter, and Susan Glasser. *Kremlin Rising: Vladimir Putin's Russia and the End of Revolution*. New York: Scribner, 2005.

Belton, Catherine. *Putin's People: How the KGB Took Back Russia and Then Took On the West*. New York: Farrar, Straus and Giroux, 2020.

Gevorkyan, Natalya, Natalya Timakova, and Andrei Kolesnikov. *Ot Pervogo Litsa: Razgovory s Vladimirom Putinym*. Moscow: Vagrius, 2000.

Goldgeier, James. "Bill and Boris: A Window Into a Most Important Post–Cold War Relationship." *Texas National Security Review* 1, no. 4 (August 2018). tnsr.org/2018/08/bill-and-boris-a-window-into-a-most-important-post-cold-war-relationship/.

Graham, Thomas. "The Putin Files: Thomas Graham." Interview by Michael Kirk. *Frontline*, June 19, 2017. pbs.org/wgbh/frontline/interview/thomas-graham/.

Hall, Steven L. "Intelligence Sharing with Russia: A Practitioner's Perspective." Carnegie Endowment for International Peace, February 9, 2017. carnegieendowment.org/2017/02/09/intelligence-sharing-with-russia-practitioner-s-perspective-pub-67962.

Hoffman, David E. *The Oligarchs: Wealth and Power in the New Russia*. New York: Public Affairs, 2011.

Keenan, Edward L. "Muscovite Political Folkways." *Russian Review* 45, no. 2 (April 1986): 115–81. jstor.org/stable/130423?origin=JSTOR-pdf.

Kotkin, Stephen. "The Resistible Rise of Vladimir Putin: Russia's Nightmare Dressed Like a Daydream." *Foreign Affairs*, March/April 2015. foreignaffairs.com/reviews/resistible -rise-vladimir-putin.

———. "Russia's Perpetual Geopolitics: Putin Returns to the Historical Pattern." *Foreign Affairs*, May/June 2016. foreignaffairs.com/articles/ukraine/2016-04-18/russias -perpetual-geopolitics.

Mlechin, Leonid. *Kreml. Prezidenty Rossii, Strategiya vlasti ot B.N. Yeltsina do V. V. Putina*. Moscow: Tsentropoligraf, 2002.

Myers, Steven Lee. *The New Tsar: The Rise and Reign of Vladimir Putin*. New York: Vintage Books, 2015.

National Security Council and NSC Records Management System. Memorandum of Telephone Conversation with Russian President Yeltsin, June 13, 1999. "Declassified Documents Concerning Russian President Boris Yeltsin." Clinton Digital Library. clinton.presidentiallibraries.us/items/show/57569.

———. Memorandum of Telephone Conversation with Russian President Yeltsin, September 8, 1999. "Declassified Documents Concerning Russian President Boris Yeltsin." Clinton Digital Library. clinton.presidentiallibraries.us/items/show/57569.

——— Memorandum of Telephone Conversation with President Putin of Russia, December 27, 2000. "Declassified Documents Concerning Russian President Vladimir Putin." Clinton Digital Library. clinton.presidentiallibraries.us/items/show/100505.

Pavlovsky, Gleb. "The Putin Files: Gleb Pavlovsky." Interview by Michael Kirk. *Frontline*, July 13, 2017. pbs.org/wgbh/frontline/interview/gleb-pavlovsky/.

Putin, Vladimir. "Rossiia na Rubezhe Tysiacheletii." *Nezavisimaya Gazeta*, December 30, 1999. ng.ru/politics/1999-12-30/4_millenium.html.

Rumer, Eugene, and Richard Sokolsky. "Etched in Stone: Russian Strategic Culture and the Future of Transatlantic Security." Carnegie Endowment for International Peace, September 8, 2020. carnegieendowment.org/2020/09/08/etched-in-stone-russian -strategic-culture-and-future-of-transatlantic-security-pub-82657.

Talbott, Strobe. "The Putin Files: Strobe Talbott." Interview by Michael Kirk. *Frontline*, June 20, 2017. pbs.org/wgbh/frontline/interview/strobe-talbott/.

———. *The Russia Hand: A Memoir of Presidential Diplomacy*. New York: Random House, 2003.

Weiss, Andrew S. "Russia: The Accidental Alliance." In *America and the World in the Age of Terror: A New Landscape in International Relations*, edited by Daniel Benjamin, 125–172. Washington, DC: CSIS Press, 2005.

———. "Tsarnaev Brothers' Impact on U.S.-Russian Counterterrorism Cooperation." *Daily Beast*. Updated July 11, 2017. thedailybeast.com/tsarnaev-brothers-impact-on-us -russian-counterterrorism-cooperation.

Yumashev, Valentin. Interview with Vladimir Posner, November 25, 2021. "Pochemy Boris Yeltsin Vybral Vladimira Putina." echo.msk.ru/programs/beseda/2542945-echo/.

CHAPTER 4

Arrow, Ruaridh, dir. *How to Start a Revolution*. The Big Indy, 2011. Transcript accessed online. mediaed.org/transcripts/How-to-Start-a-Revolution-Transcript.pdf.

Åslund, Anders, and Michael McFaul, eds. *Revolution in Orange: The Origins of Ukraine's Democratic Breakthrough*. Washington, DC: Carnegie Endowment for International Peace, 2006.

Belton, Catherine. *Putin's People: How the KGB Took Back Russia and Then Took On the West*. New York: Farrar, Straus and Giroux, 2020.

Burns, William J. *The Back Channel: A Memoir of American Diplomacy and the Case for Its Renewal*. New York: Random House, 2019.

Carothers, Thomas. "The Backlash Against Democracy Promotion." *Foreign Affairs* 85, no. 2 (March/April 2006). foreignaffairs.com/articles/2006-03-01/backlash-against -democracy-promotion.

Dobbs, Michael. "U.S. Advice Guided Milosevic Opposition." *Washington Post*, December 11, 2000. washingtonpost.com/archive/politics/2000/12/11/us-advice-guided -milosevic-opposition/ba9e87e5-bdca-45dc-8aad-da6571e89448/.

Docherty, Neil, dir. *Putin's Way*. Frontline, 2015. pbs.org/wgbh/frontline/film/putins-way/.

Furlong, Ray. "Showdown in Dresden: The Stasi Occupation and the Putin Myth." Video report, RFE/RL, December 2, 2019. rferl.org/a/showdown-in-dresden-the-stasi -occupation-and-the-putin-myth/30302831.html.

Gall, Carlotta, and Thomas de Waal. *Chechnya: Calamity in the Caucasus*. New York: NYU Press, 1998.

Gevorkyan, Natalya, Natalya Timakova, and Andrei Kolesnikov. *Ot Pervogo Litsa: Razgovory s Vladimirom Putinym*. Moscow: Vagrius, 2000.

Graham, Thomas. "The Putin Files: Thomas Graham." Interview by Michael Kirk. *Frontline*, June 19, 2017. pbs.org/wgbh/frontline/interview/thomas-graham/.

Hadley, Stephen J. "The Putin Files: Stephen Hadley." Interview by Michael Kirk. *Frontline*, July 27, 2017. pbs.org/wgbh/frontline/interview/stephen-hadley/.

Higgins, Andrew, Guy Chazan, and Alan Cullison. "Secretive Associate of Putin Emerges As Czar of Russian Oil Trading." *Wall Street Journal*, June 11, 2008. wsj.com/articles /SB121314210826662571.

Hoffman, David. "Putin Steps Out of the Shadows." *Washington Post*, January 30, 2000.

washingtonpost.com/archive/politics/2000/01/30/putin-steps-out-of-the-shadows /ca85c7c2-ebcb-4124-a9b3-4a656e877a15/.

Kondrashov, Andrei, dir. *Putin*. Nashe Kino, March 24, 2018, 4:00:00. Rossiya 24. youtube.com /watch?v=y9Pu0yrOwKI.

Laruelle, Marlene. "Commemorating 1917 in Russia: Ambivalent State History Policy and the Church's Conquest of the History Market." *Europe-Asia Studies* 71, no. 2 (2019): 249–67.

McEvers, Kelly. "'Mondrage' in Beslan: Inside the School Siege." NPR, August 31, 2006. npr.org/templates/story/story.php?storyId=5739902.

Mitchell, Lincoln A. *The Color Revolutions*. Philadelphia: University of Pennsylvania Press, 2012.

Myers, Steven Lee. *The New Tsar: The Rise and Reign of Vladimir Putin*. New York: Vintage Books, 2015.

Pavlovsky, Gleb. "The Putin Files: Gleb Pavlovsky." Interview by Michael Kirk. *Frontline*, July 13, 2017. pbs.org/wgbh/frontline/interview/gleb-pavlovsky/.

Plokhy, Serhii. *The Origins of the Slavic Nations: Premodern Identities in Russia, Ukraine, and Belarus*. Cambridge, UK: Cambridge University Press, 2006.

Putin, Vladimir. "Address by President of the Russian Federation." Transcript, March 18, 2014. en.kremlin.ru/events/president/news/20603.

Putin, Vladimir. "Putin Tells the Russians: 'We Shall Be Stronger.'" Transcript, *New York Times*, September 5, 2004. nytimes.com/2004/09/05/world/europe/putin-tells-the-russians -we-shall-be-stronger.html.

Putin, Vladimir. "Speech and the Following Discussion at the Munich Conference on Security Policy." Transcript, February 10, 2007. en.kremlin.ru/events/president /transcripts/24034.

Putin, Vladimir. "Speech at a Meeting of the Board of the Federal Security Service (FSB)." Transcript, February 7, 2006. en.kremlin.ru/events/president/transcripts/23418.

Rice, Condoleezza. *No Higher Honor: A Memoir of My Years in Washington*. New York: Broadway Paperbacks, 2012.

Rumer, Eugene, and Andrew S. Weiss. "Ukraine: Putin's Unfinished Business." Carnegie Endowment for International Peace, November 12, 2021. carnegieendowment.org /2021/11/12/ukraine-putin-s-unfinished-business-pub-85771.

Sal'ye, Marina. "Sal'ye Commission Documents." Havighurst Center for Russian and Post-Soviet Studies, Miami University. Accessed January 8, 2022. miamioh.edu/cas/academics /centers/havighurst/additional-resources/putins-russia/salye-commission-landing/index.html.

Secor, Laura. "War by Other Means." *Boston Globe*, May 29, 2005. archive.boston.com /news/globe/ideas/articles/2005/05/29/war_by_other_means?pg=full.

Shimer, David. "When the CIA Interferes in Foreign Elections: A Modern-Day History of American Covert Action." *Foreign Affairs*, June 21, 2020. foreignaffairs.com/articles /united-states/2020-06-21/cia-interferes-foreign-elections.

Stolberg, Sheryl Gay. "Shy U.S. Intellectual Created Playbook Used in a Revolution." *New York Times*, February 16, 2011. nytimes.com/2011/02/17/world/middleeast/17sharp.html.

Timchenko, Gennady. "Excerpts: Gunvor's Timchenko on His History, Putin and Gunvor." Interview by Guy Chazan. *Wall Street Journal*, June 11, 2008. wsj.com/articles /SB121313303128762055.

Tolstoy, Leo. *Hadji Murat*. Translated by Richard Pevear and Larissa Volokhonsky. New York: Vintage Classics, 2012.

Trenin, Dmitri. *Post-Imperium: A Eurasian Story*. Washington, DC: Carnegie Endowment for International Peace, 2011. carnegieendowment.org/pdf/book/post-imperium.pdf.

White, Gregory. "Russia's Sechin Defends Investment Climate." *Wall Street Journal*, February 22, 2011. wsj.com/articles/SB10001424052748704476604576158140523028546.

Wilson, Andrew. *Ukraine Crisis: What It Means for the West*. New Haven: Yale University Press, 2014.

Zykov, Andrei. "Delo Putina." Radio Svoboda, June 19, 2014. svoboda.org/a/27081099.html.

CHAPTER 5

Baker, Peter. "Pressure Rising as Obama Works to Rein In Russia." *New York Times*, March 2, 2014. nytimes.com/2014/03/03/world/europe/pressure-rising-as-obama-works-to -rein-in-russia.html?_r=1.

Baumann, Robert F. "The Decembrist Revolt and Its Aftermath: Values in Conflict." *InterAgency Journal* 10, no. 3, (2019): 21–32. thesimonscenter.org/wp-content /uploads/2019/08/IAJ-10-3-2019-pg21-32.pdf.

Bennetts, Marc. "Did Pussy Riot Destroy Russia's Anti-Putin Movement?" *Protest*, March 12, 2014. lacuna.org.uk/protest/did-pussy-riot-destroy-russias-anti-putin-movement/.

Bohm, Michael. "Putin Revives Russian Exceptionalism." *Moscow Times*, September 26, 2013. themoscowtimes.com/2013/09/26/putin-revives-russia-exceptionalism-a28048.

Chen, Adrian. "The Agency." *New York Times Magazine*, June 2, 2015. nytimes.com/2015/06 /07/magazine/the-agency.html.

Clinton, Hillary Rodham. "Remarks: Secretary of State Hillary Rodham Clinton OSCE First Plenary Session." Transcript, December 6, 2011. osce.org/files/fdocuments/4/b /85930.pdf.

Garmazhapova, Aleksandra. "Gde Zhivut Trolli. I Kto Ikh Kormit." *Novaya Gazeta*, September 9, 2013. novayagazeta.ru/articles/2013/09/07/56253-gde-zhivut-trolli-i-kto-ih-kormit.

Goldberg, Jeffrey. "The Obama Doctrine." *The Atlantic*, April 2016. theatlantic.com/magazine /archive/2016/04/the-obama-doctrine/471525/.

Gudkov, Lev. "The Technology of Negative Mobilization: Russian Public Opinion and Vladimir Putin's 'Ukrainian Policy.'" *Eurozine*, October 1, 2014. eurozine.com/the -technology-of-negative-mobilization/.

Herb, Jeremy. "Obama's Promise: No Military Action in Ukraine from US." *The Hill*, March 19, 2014. thehill.com/policy/defense/201226-obama-no-us-military-excursion-in-ukraine.

Herszenhorn, David M., and Ellen Barry. "Putin Contends Clinton Incited Unrest Over Vote." *New York Times*, December 8, 2011. nytimes.com/2011/12/09/world/europe /putin-accuses-clinton-of-instigating-russian-protests.html?_r=1.

Hosking, Geoffrey. *Russia and the Russians: A History*. Cambridge, MA: Harvard University Press, 2001.

Loiko, Sergei L. "Vladimir Putin Evokes Enemies of Russia in Campaign Speech." *Los Angeles Times*, February 24, 2012. latimes.com/world/la-xpm-2012-feb-24-la-fg -russia-putin-rally-20120224-story.html.

McFaul, Michael. *From Cold War to Hot Peace: An American Ambassador in Putin's Russia*. Boston: Mariner Books, 2019.

Menon, Rajan, and Eugene Rumer. *Conflict in Ukraine: The Unwinding of the Post–Cold War Order*. Cambridge, MA: MIT Press, 2015.

Nuland, Victoria. "The Putin Files: Victoria Nuland." Interview by Michael Kirk. *Frontline*, June 14, 2017. pbs.org/wgbh/frontline/interview/victoria-nuland/.

Pipes, Richard. *Russian Conservatism and Its Critics: A Study in Political Culture*. New Haven: Yale University Press, 2007.

Poe, Marshall. "Moscow, the Third Rome: The Origins and Transformations of a 'Pivotal Moment.'" *Jahrbücher für Geschichte Osteuropas* 49, no. 3, (2001): 412–29. jstor.org /stable/41050783.

Putin, Vladimir. "Interview to American TV Channel CBS and PBS." Transcript, September 29, 2015. en.kremlin.ru/events/president/news/50380.

Putin, Vladimir. "Meeting of the Valdai International Discussion Club." Transcript, September 19, 2013. en.kremlin.ru/events/president/news/19243.

Snyder, Timothy. "A Fascist Hero in Democratic Kiev." *New York Review of Books*, February 24, 2010. nybooks.com/daily/2010/02/24/a-fascist-hero-in-democratic-kiev/.

Travin, Dmitriy. "Teorii Osobogo Puti Rossii: Klassiki i Sovremennik." European University in St. Petersburg, Center for the Study of Modernization, 2015. eusp.org/sites/default /files/archive/M_center/M_43_15.pdf.

Weiss, Andrew S. "Winter Has Come." *Democracy: A Journal of Ideas*, no. 30 (Fall 2013). democracyjournal.org/author/asweiss/.

Wilson, Andrew. *Ukraine Crisis: What It Means for the West*. New Haven: Yale University Press, 2014.

CHAPTER 6

Annenova, Olga. "Blok Nato Razoshelsya no Blokpakety." *Kommersant*, April 7, 2008. kommersant.ru/doc/877224.

Associated Press. "Congressmen Find Few Boston Attack Clues in Russia." *Politico*, June 3, 2013. politico.com/story/2013/06/boston-bombings-russia-dana-rohrabacher-092133.

Becker, Jo, Steven Erlanger, and Eric Schmitt. "How Russia Often Benefits When Julian Assange Reveals the West's Secrets." *New York Times*, August 31, 2016. nytimes .com/2016/09/01/world/europe/wikileaks-julian-assange-russia.html?_r=2.

Blue, Miranda. "Franklin Graham Praises 'Gay Propaganda' Law, [Criticizes] US 'Secularism' in Russia Visit." *Right Wing Watch*, November 2, 2015. rightwingwatch.org/post /franklin-graham-praises-gay-propaganda-law-critizes-us-secularism-in-russia-visit/.

Burns, William J. *The Back Channel: A Memoir of American Diplomacy and the Case for Its Renewal*. New York: Random House, 2019.

Clover, Charles. *Black Wind, White Snow: The Rise of Russia's New Nationalism*. New Haven: Yale University Press, 2016.

Coker, Margaret, and Paul Sonne. "Ukraine: Cyberwar's Hottest Front." *Wall Street Journal*, November 9, 2015. wsj.com/articles/ukraine-cyberwars-hottest-front-1447121671.

Foer, Franklin. "It's Putin's World." *Atlantic*, March 2017. theatlantic.com/magazine /archive/2017/03/its-putins-world/513848/?utm_source=atltw.

Greenberg, Andy. "Here's the Evidence That Links Russia's Most Brazen Cyberattacks." *Wired*, November 15, 2019. wired.com/story/sandworm-russia-cyberattack-links/.

Helderman, Rosalind S., and Tom Hamburger. "Trump Adviser Flynn Paid by Multiple Russia–Related Entities, New Records Show." *Washington Post*, March 16, 2017. washingtonpost.com/politics/new-details-released-on-russia-related-payments-to -flynn-before-he-joined-trump-campaign/2017/03/16/52a4205a-0a55-11e7-a15f -a58d4a988474_story.html.

Higgins, Andrew. "Ukraine Upheaval Highlights E.U.'s Past Miscalculations and Future Dangers." *New York Times*, March 20, 2014. nytimes.com/2014/03/21/world/europe /ukrainian-tumult-highlights-european-unions-errors.html.

Kalugin, Oleg. "Inside the KGB: An Interview with Retired KGB Maj. Gen. Oleg Kalugin." Interview with *Cold War* production team. CNN, January 1998. web.archive.org /web/20070627183623/http://www3.cnn.com/SPECIALS/cold.war/episodes/21 /interviews/kalugin/.

Lee, Michelle Ye Hee. "Julian Assange's Claim That There Was No Russian Involvement in WikiLeaks Emails." *Washington Post*, January 5, 2017. washingtonpost.com/news /fact-checker/wp/2017/01/05/julian-assanges-claim-that-there-was-no-russian -involvement-in-wikileaks-emails/.

Mak, Tim. "Documents Reveal How Russian Official Courted Conservatives in U.S. Since 2009." NPR, May 11, 2018. npr.org/2018/05/11/610206357/documents-reveal-how -russian-official-courted-conservatives-in-u-s-since-2009.

Myers, Steven Lee. "Russia's Move into Ukraine Said to Be Born in Shadows." *New York Times*, March 7, 2014. nytimes.com/2014/03/08/world/europe/russias-move-into -ukraine-said-to-be-born-in-shadows.html.

On the Issues. "Jill Stein on Foreign Policy." Accessed January 8, 2022. ontheissues. org/2016/Jill_Stein_Foreign_Policy.htm.

Osborn, Andrew, and William James. "UK's Anti-EU Leader Accused of Being Apologist for Russia Before Vote." *Reuters*, March 27, 2014. reuters.com/article/us-ukraine-crisis -britain-politics/uks-anti-eu-leader-accused-of-being-apologist-for-russia-before -vote-idUSBREA2Q16A20140327.

Putin, Vladimir. "All This Fuss About Spies . . . It Is Not Worth Serious Interstate Relations." Transcript, *Financial Times*, June 27, 2019. ft.com/content/878d2344-98f0-11e9-9573 -ee5cbb98ed36.

Rid, Thomas. *Active Measures: The Secret History of Disinformation and Political Warfare.* New York: Farrar, Straus and Giroux, 2020.

RT. "US 'Rudely and Insolently Cheated Russia' During Ukraine Coup —Putin." March 8, 2018. rt.com/news/420785-ukraine-coup-us-putin/.

Sonne, Paul. "A Russian Bank Gave Marine Le Pen's Party a Loan. Then Weird Things Began Happening." *Washington Post*, December 27, 2018. washingtonpost.com/world /national-security/a-russian-bank-gave-marine-le-pens-party-a-loan-then-weird-things -began-happening/2018/12/27/960c7906-d320-11e8-a275-81c671a50422_story.html.

Stein, Jeff. "A Conversation with Jill Stein: What the Green Party Candidate Believes." *Vox*, September 14, 2016. vox.com/2016/9/14/12913174/jill-stein-green-party.

United States District Court for the District of Columbia. "United States' Memorandum in Aid of Sentencing." United States of America v. Maria Butina, April 19, 2019. s3.documentcloud.org/documents/5972875/4-19-19-US-Sentencing-Memo-Butina.pdf.

U.S. Department of Justice. "Report on the Investigation into Russian Interference in the 2016 Presidential Election, Volume I of II." March 2019. justice.gov/archives/sco /file/1373816/download.

U.S. Senate Committee on Finance Minority Staff Report. "The NRA and Russia: How a Tax-Exempt Organization Became a Foreign Asset." September 2019. finance .senate.gov/imo/media/doc/The%20NRA%20%20Russia%20-%20How%20a%20Tax -Exempt%20Organization%20Became%20a%20Foreign%20Asset.pdf.

Weiss, Andrew S. "Vladimir Putin's Political Meddling Revives Old KGB Tactics." *Wall Street Journal*, February 17, 2017. wsj.com/articles/vladimir-putins-political-meddling -revives-old-kgb-tactics-1487368678.

Zygar, Miwkhail. *All the Kremlin's Men: Inside the Court of Vladimir Putin.* New York: Public Affairs, 2016.

———. "The Putin Files: Mikhail Zygar." Interview by Michael Kirk. *Frontline*, June 20, 2017. pbs.org/wgbh/frontline/interview/mikhail-zygar/.

ACKNOWLEDGMENTS

Working on this book has been a singular experience that brought home to me just how lucky I have been over the course of a thirty-plus-year career to learn from so many of the world's best Russia experts.

Yet one thing has been clear since I enrolled in an introductory Russian language course as a first-year student at Columbia University in autumn 1986. Nearly every single day I have been humbled by the limitations of what I could ever possibly hope to know about a country as complex as Russia.

My biggest intellectual debt is owed to the scores of people with whom I served in different parts of the U.S. government as well as to my colleagues at the Carnegie Endowment for International Peace's offices in Washington, D.C., and Moscow.

Since 2013, I have been fortunate to call Carnegie home. The Endowment's leadership during the period when this book was written—Ambassador Bill Burns, Thomas Carothers, and Elizabeth Dibble—gave me support and intellectual freedom unlike anything I've experienced at any point in my career.

I am deeply grateful to Brian Brown for his willingness to partner up with a comics neophyte. Brian's artistic vision and his own graphic novels have been a source of inspiration and flat-out awe.

Getting this project off the ground would not have been possible without the fierce enthusiasm of Mark Siegel at First Second; my agent, Tanya McKinnon; and my close friend Marc Favreau.

Alex Lu and the entire team at First Second were terrific partners in the editing and production of this book.

I relied on a wide array of English- and Russian-language source material for the book, plus informal conversations with a great number of Russian and Western colleagues, experts, and officials over the years.

One can easily assemble a large library of books about Putin and Russia during his rule. *The New Tsar: The Rise and Reign of Vladimir Putin* by Steven Lee Myers, the former Moscow bureau chief of the *New York Times*, is, for my money, still the most comprehensive Putin biography in English. I found myself returning to it over and over. Other key source material included works by Catherine Belton, Fiona Hill and Clifford G. Gaddy, Masha Gessen, and Mikhail Zygar.

Several friends and colleagues provided reactions to the manuscript, including Chris Bort, Michael Kimmage, Robert Otto, Eugene Rumer, Mary Sarotte, Alex Star, and Paul Stronski. Aleksandar Vladicic fact-checked the book with much-needed fresh eyes. Grace Kier, who like Aleks is a former Carnegie junior fellow, provided outstanding research assistance. Any remaining errors of fact or judgment are mine alone.

Finally, I would be nowhere without the love (and reservoirs of patience) of my wife, Kate Julian, and our two children, Clara and Caleb (whose enthusiasm for Harry Potter arcana inspired the subtitle).

This book is dedicated to them.

—**ANDREW S. WEISS**

Special thanks to everyone at First Second, as well as James Kochalka, Meghan Turbitt, Pat Aulisio, Ian Harker, Sarah B., Eugene B., and Archie B.

—**BRIAN "BOX" BROWN**

ANDREW S. WEISS is the James Family chair and vice president for studies at the Carnegie Endowment for International Peace in Washington, D.C., where he oversees research on Russia and Eurasia. He served in various policy roles at the National Security Council, the State Department, and the Pentagon during both Democratic and Republican administrations. His writings have appeared in the *New York Times*, the *Washington Post*, the *Wall Street Journal*, *Foreign Affairs*, and other publications. He and his wife, Kate Julian, have two children.

BRIAN "BOX" BROWN is an Eisner Award–winning comic artist and illustrator living in Philadelphia. His comics have appeared in the *New York Times*, *Playboy*, and *New York Magazine*. His books include the *New York Times*-bestselling *Andre the Giant: Life and Legend*, *Tetris: The Games People Play*, *Is This Guy for Real?: The Unbelievable Andy Kaufman*, *Cannabis: The Illegalization of Weed in America*, and *Child Star*. His strip *Legalization Nation* is updated weekly.

AFTERWORD

AS THIS BOOK GOES TO PRESS, RUSSIAN FORCES HAVE ENCIRCLED Ukraine's major cities and are pummeling civilian targets indiscriminately. Democracies around the world have responded forcefully and with great speed. Ukraine's elected government remains in power, and its citizens are fighting back with unmatched courage and resourcefulness. But they are badly outnumbered, and defeat may be inevitable.

Putin's actions have reordered international relations to an extent not seen since the 9/11 attacks. But we don't know yet whether this reordering will mean a new cold war with countries once again divided into two armed camps, or something even more precarious. We do know that the whims of one man will shape whether we experience war or peace in the years ahead.

For someone whose KGB career stalled out at the rank of lieutenant colonel, Putin has, to put it mildly, outperformed. But in a plot worthy of Sophocles or Shakespeare, his invasion of Ukraine has now set in motion his own worst nightmare. Putin has long feared ending up like former Yugoslav president Slobodan Milošević, who died in prison while being tried for war crimes in The Hague. Following the color revolutions of the 2000s and 2010s, Putin also grew obsessed with the possibility of the West trying to oust him. This chapter seems unlikely to have a happy ending for anyone—certainly not for the countless Ukrainians who have died or fled; not for the Russians trapped under Putin's repressive regime; and not even for those of us lucky enough to live in other countries. The world is waking up to the reality that Putin was never the master strategist he made himself out to be. He is an improviser who has stumbled into a trap he built all by himself.

—**ANDREW S. WEISS**,
March 2022, Washington, D.C.